DON'T LOOK DOWN

DON'T LOOK
DOWN

Learning how to live a fearless life
by taking courageous steps of faith and
finding hope along the way

DENISE AMIRANTE

DON'T LOOK
DOWN

Learning how to live a fearless life by taking
courageous steps of faith and finding hope
along the way

DENISE AMIRANTE

Table of Contents

Introduction

Every non-fiction book tells a real story, and the Bible is no different. From the beginning of its historic pages when God created the heavens and the Earth to the fall of man to the death and resurrection of Jesus Christ and the future prophetic judgment of the seven churches, God breathed His written word through Holy Spirit-inspired men. His story was penned for the whole world to read 2,000 years ago.

God made it very clear in the beginning through His written Word that He exists. He also made it clear that Satan exists. Not only do both exist, but both have a plan for our lives. In the Gospel of John, Jesus tells us, "The thief (Satan) comes only to steal and kill and destroy; I (Jesus) came that they may have life and have it abundantly." (John 10:10 ESV) Satan knows he can't destroy God, but he can destroy what God has created, and that means you and me. And he will go to every extreme to accomplish his ends. In an interview with Larry King in 2005, Billy Graham stated, "There are two great forces, God's force of good and the devil's force of evil, and I believe Satan is alive, and he is working, and he is working harder than ever, and we have many mysteries that we don't understand." Below is the story of how Satan came into the world and remains in the world that we live in today.

Who is Lucifer

It all started out pretty nicely in heaven when God created His most beautiful angel above all other angels and named him Lucifer. Lucifer was the most adorned angel in heaven. He was God's chief angel, covered in gold and all kinds of jewels from head to toe. He was literally an instrument with harps, a tambourine, and the flute, all a part of his own body. The prophet Ezekiel reflects, "You were the seal of perfection, full of wisdom and perfect in beauty. You were in Eden, the garden of God; every precious stone was your covering: the sardius, topaz, diamond, beryl, onyx, jasper, sapphire, turquoise, and emerald with gold. The workmanship of your timbrels and pipes was prepared for you on the day you were created. You were the anointed cherub who covers; I established you; You were on the holy mountain of God; You walked back and forth in the midst of the fiery stones." (Ezekiel 28:12-14 NKJV) Satan was an instrument of music, most likely the director of music created to make music to worship God.

The Pride

All was well in Lucifer's world until he wanted to be just like God. It wasn't enough to be God's angel above all angels. No. Lucifer wanted more power, and he didn't stop going after it. Well, that only lasted for so long before God had no choice but to take action. Satan's greed for control persisted until finally, God was left with no other choice except to throw him out of heaven.

Ezekiel also compares Satan's pride with that of the prince of Tyre. "Your heart became proud on account of your beauty, and you corrupted your wisdom because of your splendor." (Ezekiel 28:17 NIV) Satan's pride was his greatest downfall. Lucifer wasn't the only one thrown out of heaven. Along with him went one-third of the angels that followed him. And guess where they ended up? That's right, here on Earth. At that point in history, Lucifer's name was changed to Satan. The Earth is Satan's domain. This is how Satan ended up in the garden with Adam and Eve.

The Perfect Life

When God made Adam and Eve in His image, they were the perfect people, had a perfect relationship with God, and lived in a perfect place. That all changed when Satan entered the picture. At the time of creation, God gave Adam and Eve one command: "…but you must not eat from the tree of the knowledge of good and evil, for when you eat from it, you will certainly die." (Genesis 2:17 NIV) God was not talking about a physical death but a spiritual death. God gave Adam and Eve the gift of free will, and it was that very gift that led them outside of the boundary lines of God's grace and protection. Although God gave them everything they would ever need, they still wanted more than God offered them.

The Fall

Satan opposed the very word of God and told Eve, "You will not certainly die." (Genesis 3:4 NIV) Eve listened to the voice of Satan over God's voice and was curious as to what would actually happen if she ate from the fruit. This is where the fall comes in. On the day when Eve took the first bite of the fruit from the tree, sin was born into the world. Everything that was once made perfect became broken, and with sin came fierce repercussions that the whole world would begin to face. Death is now introduced to the world and mankind.

Today, this is why there is every form of rebelliousness against God. Billy Graham said, "Death wasn't part of God's original plan for humanity, and the Bible calls death an enemy—the last enemy to be destroyed." Satan is known as the prince of this world. Be careful that you are not so ignorant of his ways to the point that you turn your back on the God who made you in His image. Peter tells us, "...the god of this world has blinded the minds of the unbelieving so that they might not see the light of the gospel of the glory of Christ, who is the image of God." (2 Corinthians 4:4) Satan is the reason evil exists, God is not.

The Warning

When Satan was thrown out of heaven, he didn't get a second chance to get it right as we do through Jesus, and he is extremely unhappy about that! Satan has a counterfeit for everything God does. He will twist and pervert the word of God until we become deceived by him and eventually make choices in our lives that reflect his perversion. In the same way, God works in and through us, Satan also works in and through us *if* we allow him to. Satan cannot get inside our hearts; only God can do that. However, Satan works through our minds and has the power to harden our hearts which can influence the choices we make. Jesus warns us of Satan in John 8:

> "If God were your Father, you would love me, for I came from God, and I am here. I came not of my own accord, but He sent me. Why do you not understand what I say? It is because

you cannot bear to hear my word. You are of your father, the devil, and your will is to do your father's desires. He was a murderer from the beginning and does not stand in the truth because there is no truth in him. When he lies, he speaks out of his own character, for he is a liar and the father of lies. But because I tell the truth, you do not believe me. Which one of you convicts me of sin? If I tell the truth, why do you not believe me? Whoever is of God hears the words of God. The reason why you do not hear them is that you are not of God." (John 8:42-47 ESV)

The Conclusion

Satan, hell, and evil exist. No wishing it away, thinking good thoughts, or sending good vibes, will make Satan's vicious and wicked schemes disappear. He preys on the weak, the lonely, and the lost. He preys on little children. He preyed on me.

I pray my story opens the eyes of your heart, teaches you how to find hope that gives you the strength to make the right choices in your life, and gives you an understanding of the love of God that can change your world today and forevermore.

Blessings to you all!

Denise

"Let the redeemed of the LORD
tell their story –
those He redeemed
from the hand of the foe."
(Psalm 107:2)

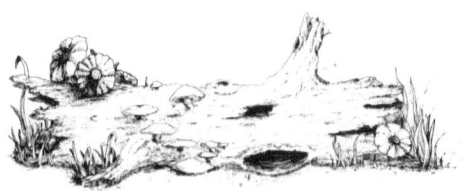

Chapter 1
The Playroom

"Hope has two beautiful daughters; their names are Anger and Courage. Anger at the way things are and Courage to see that they do not remain as they are."
- Saint Augustine

When I was a little girl, my mother told me I always used to say, "Lee me 'lone." It wasn't until I was somewhere in my late 20s that we both realized I was sexually abused by a great Uncle. The first feather plucks out hard, and I swirl around like a wingless bird losing sky.

The money machine sat on the bamboo-legged coffee table. There was a permanent fixture of city smog meeting summer days in June, the sun hanging high on the shoulder of God. July flags were unrolled proud, and the twirling of sparklers in little hands lit up smiles at dusk. It was the rolling of tires up the gravel drive giving city smog a breath of country air. And on that day, beaming light wakes dead places beyond the wood-paneled walls of the playroom downstairs.

His wrinkles, filthy, clutched the black handle like he was clutching my heart. The cranking of it slowly and steadily squeezed out the one-dollar bill and the breath in me.

Upstairs in the kitchen, my mother was keeping step with the band of the pots and pans. The clinking and clunking of metal and glass were like a Broadway musical preparing a banquet for the six of us kids and our hungry father. He was her King, and she was his Fair Lady. His place was always at the head of the table, and hers always to the right of him. Every night we would all bow our noses into plates and give glorious thanks to God for Thy bounty about to fill our empty. And when our voices rang out a blaring "Amen," there we went barging in with forks to meat like wolves on dead skin. We were a holy mess under that rooftop at times, but a mess we've all grown accustomed to.

Every night was like a faithful song. King would lift his glass of very bad wine and kiss his Fair Lady's glass with a ding and declare his "I love you." Fair Lady answered a soft "I love you back," and they would sip in slow the woes of the day and the bills high as heaven. It was the hearing of the "I love you" that stitched them together during the hard and angry years. It was holding tight to the American dream during scarce years that tucked us kids snug into bed every night. It was never knowing what was going on behind closed doors. As hard as things got, we kids never saw them argue. Never. We only saw the love between them.

I could hear the unwrapping of the paper that held the butter safe and secure in its salty-sweet and the dropping of it in the small pot for the melting.

Butter sizzles like a zipper unzipping.

Downstairs I lay unzipped on the couch right under my mother's heel. The sweetness of my spirit was about to come unwrapped. My small was about to melt into the slip-covered cushions. He placed his body on top of me, and in that moment, little did I know, the slow freeze that would last for years to come would begin right there where my innocence was undone.

I. Was. Undone.

And so, Satan gets thrown out of heaven and lands right there on top of me? How did this happen? I didn't do anything wrong. I just go downstairs to use the bathroom, and he walks in on me! I froze and said I'll be right out. What was I supposed to say? I always lock bathroom doors now. I come out, and there he is, this old, wrinkled person who smells, standing in my way. I think of Jesus hanging on splintered wood for me in that moment. I bet if he could, he would've gotten off of that cross to save me, but that was the whole point of the crucifixion. Jesus did it to save me.

I grew to hate that stupid money machine that he traveled with. He can't just give me a dollar and expect me to be his. What an idiot. In the Garden of Eden, that would never happen before the two of them sinned. So, I guess everything's a game. Because of sin, I had this person on top of me. Dirty socks, mothballs, and dust. That's what he smelled like.

I lost my voice that day; tiny as it was, it was gone. When you don't know how to speak, you become a good listener, and that's what I became. I am a good listener.

Fear began to take the space of every broken place. My emotional growth was stunted from that moment on. Fear piled up in me like a giant mountain blocking any ray of light from my heart's eyes. A chilling presence occupied the space around me for a long, long time, and sometimes even still, when I am in the presence of men who hold some type of authority.

The weight of his sin pressed down hard on my innocence. If there was ever a time I wished I was in a movie, this was it. I would love to be someone else right now.

"Shhh," he said.

My eyes were like glue stuck on the ceiling above me where my mother walked from sink to stove.

Sink. Stove. Sink. Stove.

Up and down he goes—all wobbly on top of me. I'm surprised he didn't fall off that couch. But if he did, I'd of made a run for it right up those stairs straight to my mother's thigh.

And in a dream, my arms reach up through ceiling clouds into heaven's kitchen floor. Tiny fingers hold hard onto warm ankles like a safe hook to hang my rescue on. Like Jesus hanging on to that cross, holding on to every word of God. Why have you forsaken us? I pull my mother's ankles down close to me through the clouds hugging me away to the backyard swing set. And my mother pushes me up to the sun where God is. And we laugh. And my toes touch the baby blue. And we laugh some more. Then one big push and I lift off my swing seat into the hands of God secure around my waist. And we play, and God tells me He loves me. And God throws me up into the sun and back down into His arms I come. Up into the sun and back down into his arms. Up and down.

Up. Down. Sink. Stove.

"Does that feel good?" old wrinkles asked.

My mother grabs the pan with the chicken in it. The faucet is running cold, washing the chicken clean and splashing the wings. The drumsticks are in melted butter, ready for the breading of the crumbs. My mother made the best bread-crumbed chicken. She knew it was my favorite. That and roast beef real red.

Suddenly, I hear the suction of the refrigerator door open, and the life is sucked out of me. It was as if a mini tornado had touched down in the center of me. Unlike anything I had ever felt before. The 'little' sucked out. Right then. Like ripples in the ocean running through my body. Right there on those slip-covered cushions. I am afraid.

Gumby falls from my tiny grip bouncing rubber eyes staring up at me. Gumby, scared and hurting, needs me, but I can't reach him, so our eyes hold each other tight where we are. Safe and long eyes open wide, waiting for it to stop. I float away in search of the yellow bricks and the slippers ruby now scuffed up in my head. And I click, and I click, and I want to go home because there's no place like it. But I am home, and I don't want to be here right now.

And then it clicks. Something clicks in me.

I am broken.

He. Broke. Me.

God, are you there?

My small imagination split away from the wood-paneled walls surrounding me to my pretend. And I stare out the window because I want to be free. And the frog under the porch leaped up and down near the cobwebs free in the dirt, eating the dead bugs and the spiders. And off he goes with his frog belly full on his way to the willow tree where the summer shade slows his tiny frog heart down. And I bet his soft belly bottom feels cool resting on the willow leaves fallen fluffed up like a blanket on the grass. And I wish he wouldn't have left so soon. If I could, I would ride on his back and rest under that willow tree with him.

A lie like a seed, Satan's seed, buried itself inside me on that day. All the unworthiness and insecurities and fear as big as the green giant made a home inside my head where little people started to live. There were no pigtails and ponies or puppies and princes. Just a dream of a wedding dress locked up in a dusty old dirty coffin with no light and no key.

Every open prayer, open dream, and open voice shut down. That was it. That was when I shut down. And I wonder why me? Why anyone? I wondered if all little girls do this. What did I do wrong? Why did I deserve this? I didn't know what was happening, but I knew inside of my little mind that this wasn't right. I lay there looking up and promised myself I would forget it all. And so, I did—for years.

The screen door pulls open strong, and my father is home from work.

Old wrinkles lifted his old devil body off of my tiny one. "Don't tell anyone," he said.

My father saves me. A declaration I would come to realize has eternal value later in life.

11

MY. FATHER. SAVES. ME.

"Kids, come set the table," my mother yells out to any of us who will listen.

I race up those black banisters as quickly as my little legs can run. I stand right next to my mother by the stove with arms circled around her warm, begging for her love like the blanket she knit for me years later that begged for the defrost. I wonder if she feels the cold.

I say, "I don't want to be an actress like everyone else. I want to help people."

My mother says, "Oh, honey, you won't make any money doing that." And so, I became an actress.

The *Very* Good News

There is a saying, 'the damage is done,' but I am here to tell you the damage is never done because Jesus didn't stay in the grave. When Jesus rose from the dead, every abuse you and I would ever face in our lives was healed by the blood he shed for us. God sent Jesus into the world to fix broken things, heal broken hearts, and mend broken minds. The end result of sexual abuse doesn't dictate our worth. You and I are worth the life of Jesus, that was given as a sacrificial offering for our redemption! Jesus gave his life because you and I are worth it! Satan wants to *harm* us to the point of debilitation, but the very good news is God wants to restore us back to a place of hope and wholeness for the future he holds for us through Jesus.

"For I know the plans I have for you," declares the LORD, "plans to prosper you and not the harm you, plans to give you hope and a future."

(Jeremiah 29:11 NIV)

Chapter 2

Tennessee Jesus

"Pain insists upon being attended to. God whispers to us in our pleasures, speaks in our consciences, but shouts in our pains. It is His megaphone to rouse a deaf world." - C. S. Lewis

When I was a little girl, I had a short yet poignant conversation with my father. We were sitting on our plastic-covered gold and cream striped couch in the living room when I turned to him and said, "I feel different from the other kids." My father said, "What do you mean, different?" I said, "There's a lightbulb over my head, and it goes with me wherever I go. I don't know if people can see it when they look at me." My father replied with absolute certainty, "That is the light of the Lord." This was the first vision of many I would begin to have in my life.

I was the saddest girl anyone ever knew. It wasn't until later in my life, when I realized I had been sexually abused, that I understood why severe depression and suicidal thoughts were a part of my everyday life. I was raised Catholic, but the sad fact is that the Catholic faith didn't tell me how to have a relationship with Jesus. My Catholic faith kept Jesus on the cross. I was bleeding in the pew, and no one ever saw—no one but Jesus from the cross. And the distance from me to Him was just too wide. I tried everything from psychics and tarot cards to a short stint with Buddha to cocaine and alcohol, only to be filled with emptiness. I wanted to be used by God, yet, I couldn't figure out why He hated me. I didn't know what being a sinner was or that I was one. This was my spiritual existence.

My mother used to say to me, "Denise, you have to love yourself. You have to love you." It was as if she was speaking in a different language. I spent most of my life figuring out how to love myself. I mean, how does anyone love themselves? Is there an instruction book? Is there a button to push somewhere inside me? I never quite grasped what she meant. All her life, she whispered in my ear in different volumes trying to get the right response from me, but I'm afraid I never got it right while she was here on this side of heaven. I think about her all the time. Deep down, I think I inherited her strength to go on. Maybe that was part of it. The loving me thing and standing strong during the storms of life. I got that from her. So, maybe, just maybe, I loved myself strong because of who she was and how fearless she really was. My mother had a survival mechanism built into her. I wish I had that then. I think I have a bit of that now. I began to have visions all the time. Before she passed, God showed me the hospital room she was staying in. I told her when we were talking on the phone where everything was in the room. I told her there was an angel in the far-right corner. I'll never forget that call. We prayed.

✳✳✳

I was very close to my youngest brother, Tommy. For different reasons, we shared common feelings of deep depression and confided in each other a lot. We had a closeness that was very special. Although I loved all my brothers and sisters, and each relationship was unique in its own way, my relationship with Tommy was growing in the same way at that time. It was as if our spirits longed for the same thing. A kind of love. A love that was bigger than the world could give, and we bonded deeply because of it. *When we long for the same things, we are drawn to the same things.*

> *When we long for the same things, we are drawn to the same things.*

There was a time when we both had no idea what we wanted to do with our lives. I remember us having a conversation saying if God would just tell us what to do, we would do it! I saw myself as an introvert at times and never imagined I would end up in television and film just a few years later. However, the camera always felt like home to me. I was drawn to it like a magnet. Crowds, on the other hand, scared me to death. The thought of getting up in front of an audience would make my body freeze. I was like an ice cube, afraid to melt at the thought of having to sing a song in front of people gaping at me. It took years before I would step on a stage. And when I finally did, I was years too late for what I thought at the time God wanted to do. I'll never forget singing Karaoke at a bar in Studio City, California. When I was finished singing, and while the crowd applauded loudly, a man came up to the stage and said, "If you don't sing, you will be committing the biggest sin in your life!" He scared the crap out of me! At that point, I was still working through the fear of not only singing, but I was also so intimidated by the thought of singing in front of certain people. Mostly those who were controlling or authoritative. It was only because my friend, Adel, believed in me and wouldn't let me not sing that I sang. I think she was my biggest fan. She was the one who really wanted to sing and just dragged me along with her.

The Waitressing Job

Tommy and I were eating at Mama Mia's one night, and he bet me that I wouldn't get a waitressing job. And so, I did! I got a job at the tourist trap and very popular Nashville Palace, where several country stars like Randy Travis found their way. The band leader, Steve Hill, would call the waiters up to sing throughout the night. Well, every night when he was getting ready to call a name, I would hide in the bathroom or run out to my car, so afraid he would call me. Sometimes I would stay gone for at least fifteen minutes. My tables were literally waiting for me! My tables hated me. I lay in bed each night and cried, asking God to forgive me for what seemed like seventy times seven. I told Him I was going to try again the next night. Finally, after about six months of hiding and calling my mother every night to tell her I had let God down, I did it. One night, Steve came to me and said it's time for you to sing. I'm going to call you tonight. I stood in front of him and mustered up a shaky OK. The kind that echo's in the back of your throat. My greatest fear was that I would open my mouth to sing, and nothing would come out. It was that dang fear instilled in me years ago.

When Steve called me, I was a bit wobbly walking up there. It was a big stage, and I never sang with a band before. What the heck did I get myself into?! The more I kept walking, the closer I got to exposing my fear. God save me! It was all my brother's fault! It was too late to run to my car. Everyone could see me now. Even the employees and the cooks from the kitchen lined up on that wall and were watching. The notes of the song started to play, and I grabbed the mic. I opened my mouth, and all the butterflies in my stomach joined wings. I rang out the first few words, and like a miracle, it all just started to flow like a waterfall. It was a dream.

I was set free from the fear that held me back all this time. A peace came over me with every note, and I was singing in front of a couple of hundred people as if I had done it all my life.

It's funny how the things we fear are the very things that set us free. I thought about that nasty devil and how he influences us and sneaks his nasty thoughts into our minds until we believe his lies. He can't get into our hearts. But he can surely harden our hearts if we believe the lies he tells us about ourselves and about God. He loves putting God up against us. Satan filled my mind with fear until I became immobile. *But the truth is fear doesn't really exist unless we give it a place.* The world loves to shove fear in our faces until all we see is black. God did not create fear, ever. Fear is a tactic from Satan himself to keep us from doing what God has called us to do. One of Jesus' followers, Timothy, states, "God did not give us a spirit of fear, but of power and of love and of a sound mind." (2 Timothy 1:7 NKJV) The darkest fear is defeated by implementing "dunamis" faith. Prayer is our greatest weapon. In months to come, that stage became my playground. I sang Trisha Yearwood's Down on my Knees.

The Eucharist

God had been drawing me to him at an early age. As long ago as I can remember, I had a longing inside me that wanted to know Him on a deep level. I wanted to be as close to Him as I possibly could be, but I didn't know how to do that. We went to church on Saturday nights instead of Sunday mornings sometimes. Once after we received communion, when I returned to my pew, I did what I thought was a bright idea. I knelt down to pray, and instead of swallowing the eucharist, I slipped it into my hand and put it in my coat pocket. I put God in my pocket.

When I got home, I put the eucharist in a small empty white box and hid it in the back of one of the drawers in my dresser. One day when I took it out to talk to God, my mother walked in and asked what I was doing. I told her I was talking to God. She wasn't happy when she realized I had taken the eucharist home. She immediately took it from me. I really didn't know what I did wrong or what the big deal was, but that didn't stop God from giving me the desire to feel Him near. I always wondered what she did with that eucharist. I bet she thought it was a good idea, too, and kept it for herself! I'll never know. I suppose she just threw it away. But we can't just throw God away! He's too big for any trash can, and I learned He is alive no matter how much we think we can push Him away or take Him out of our lives. God is love, and who would want to throw love away? These are questions that went through my mind and the answers I learned years later. I learned that when we look for Him truthfully, with every ounce of our hearts and minds, we will find Him. Not just any god. The real one. *When we seek Him in truth, He shows up stunningly and happily excited to reveal all of His colors to us.* He has a color for each of our moody moods. *God knows us like the back of His hands and can see through the holes those Roman soldiers put through Him all the way to the holes in our hearts where* only He can fit.

only He can fit.

Visage

I was living in New York City, pursuing an acting career and doing stunt work while bartending at *Visage*, one of the hottest clubs in the city at the time. That's where I met one of my best friends. Her name was Donna Nelson, at the time, now Donna Davidson. Donna was Jewish, and God was a miracle worker. We were both lost and had no idea God was pursuing us or that, years later, we would become fierce friends in the fight for our faith. Back then, we wore skimpy gray skirts and danced around that dance floor and behind bars, all the while pouring poison down the throats of lost souls who were trying to fill themselves up with the high life, however temporary it was. Now we wear shiny headgear and armor and carry swords and shields around with us to trample on serpents and such. That serpent in the garden has nothing on us now. Oh, and there was Gil. Gilbert Brenton. He was something special. We wove in and out of each other's lives through the years but never did date as people date with roses and chocolate and all the fun of sharing families on holidays. Oh, but that Gil! I'd leave it at infatuation that could have been more if the timing was right. But why waste time if it's not God's?

I managed to get through dark days while hiding my depression from anyone who looked into my eyes. I was good at hiding. I was doubting my gifts and wondering what they actually were while conversing with my friend, Jonathan Watkins. I love that boy! In a moment of feeling rejected, Jonathan said, "You have the gift of beauty. Beauty is a gift from God." It was a gift because I did nothing to get it. In my younger days, the only thing I was ever told was that I was pretty. I was never told I had a particular talent, at least not in those days. And pretty never hit the mark. Pretty opened doors, but I had to find a way to keep those doors open. When you have no confidence in anything you do, eventually, those doors close. For some reason, if you're born pretty, people think everything is always perfect. Expectations are always high. The problem was that I never felt good enough. I was bad. And I felt bad, and nothing made that change.

So, even on my worst days, I started thinking at least I have 'pretty.' God gives us gifts to glorify him. I sure hope I get to glorify Him with the gifts He has given me once I figure out what they are. I know one thing. *I don't have to worry about not being good enough anymore because God is enough.*

The Nashville Trip

Tommy was attending Belmont College in Nashville, Tennessee. I just finished working on the movie *Married To The Mob* and took the train to Carmel to visit my parents. Carmel was a small town with no ocean. There was a lake, however. Lake Gleneida and the Shilling's lived on top of a hill that overlooked the whole thing. Today, I call it Shilling's Hill because I think the whole clan of them lives there now. One night, in my parent's kitchen, Tommy and I had a conversation over the phone. As we talked about this and that, I noticed something was different about him. I heard something different in his voice that I had never heard before. I heard hope. Tommy's voice glistened over the airwaves with pure hope that was bright like the sun. *Hope nudged the sleepy, saddened, dark side in me into something on the edge of possible change.* I wanted to change the world, but first, I had to change myself, and I didn't know how to do that. Oh, but that hope!

Hope. Spoke.

In the words he spoke, and in the silence he breathed, there was hope. The sound of hope reached me all the way from Nashville, Tennessee, to the kitchen table we ate our meals on in Carmel, New York. And I wanted to keep it. I wanted to hold it. If I could only package it up and put it in my pocket and take it everywhere I went, I would. I at least wanted to know where he got it from because I wanted it too. I was determined to have it for myself, so I booked a flight to Nashville.

Tommy and I didn't have much time alone on my visit because his school schedule was demanding. But God made a way because that's what God does, and a miracle happened on the last morning of my trip. Whether it was due to bad weather or a class being canceled, God allowed time for us to, well, do the thing I was *hoping* to do on the trip. I was looking for the hope I heard on that phone call. We were sitting in the corner of his bedroom on the floor, and just like that, I broke. I told him I couldn't do this anymore. I wanted to die and even had some sort of a plan. My eyes overflowed with buckets of fear and sadness that the little girl in me held onto all these years. It was like God was calling each teardrop by name, beckoning them to come to Him; fear, depression, loneliness, death, anxiety, unworthiness, unloveliness, and so on until they all landed in the palm of His hands.

And I blame it all on that devil. I do. All of it. Because he wanted more than he was entitled to, I had to live in a fallen state. If Satan was the one who got thrown out of heaven, why was I the one who had to feel the aftermath? I wasn't the one who wanted to be like God. I wasn't the one who wasn't satisfied with my status in life. But I'm the one, and you are too. We are the ones who have to live in an imperfect place with an imperfect relationship with God. If I could kick the devil in his you-know-what, I would. I'd like to tell him to go to hell, where he belongs. I'd use the worst words I could think of to get him there.

And that Eve, she was the one who gave into the devil's temptation and got Adam to follow right along! How stupid and selfish could they be? I guess as stupid and selfish as me when I prance down a road I shouldn't be prancing down. But they started it. Didn't they? They started the whole sin thing. When Adam and Eve sinned, we all sinned along with them. If there was anything in life that wasn't fair, that wasn't! But when you think about it, it wasn't fair to God either. God created the heavens and the Earth for you and me to live in. He didn't need it. He had heaven. He even said it was good. And He then took the time to make Adam from the dust of the Earth and later took Eve from one of his ribs; he said it was good. Male and female, He not only made the perfect couple, but He made mankind in His image! The author of Genesis, whom some believe was Moses tells us, "So God created mankind in his own image, in the image of God he created them; male and female he created them." (Genesis 1:27 NKJV) There was nothing that God created that wasn't good. And when He was finished, not only did God think His creation was good, but He added a 'very' to it, "God saw that all he had made was *very good...*" (Genesis 1:31 NIV)

The Garden of Eden was supposed to stretch out into all the world and become even more beautiful as time passed. And Adam and Eve were never supposed to die. Even though Adam and Eve sinned against God's command, that doesn't negate the truth that you and I innately have the capacity to know and love God because we are all made in His image. Now that's something to think about. We all get to start life on a clean slate if we want to. *God doesn't need us to applaud His creation. He needs us to glorify Him in it.* C. S. Lewis states, "The Christian does not think God will love us because we are good, but that God will make us good because He loves us." God loves us, and for that reason alone, I am on a long road called hope.

God doesn't need us to applaud His creation. He needs us to glorify Him in it.

My brother reached out, wrapped his arms around me, and later told me that he asked God to tell him what to say because he had no idea what to say on his own. He had no idea he was about to speak life into my dead bones. And so, he held me, and he held me some more. And then he let me go, and I know now it was the Holy Spirit who spoke through him. I can't remember the exact words he said to me, but I know they were inspired by God. Every word carried a truth and a certainty that I had never heard before, and I believed them. Each word was full of life enough to fill the emptiest parts of me.

My brother was speaking words that brought a sparkle to my saddened eyes. There was something beyond me, yet inside of me, about to be awakened. Something that was somewhere in the future that I could look forward to. It was like the tears rolled back up my cheeks, and somehow I mustered up the faith to believe everything was going to be better, at least as far as I could see. Tommy gave me a book to read called Power For

Living by Jamie Buckingham to take home with me. Jesus wasn't a stranger to me. I knew He died and rose from the dead, but I didn't see how that applied to my life or why He was the only way to get to God. (John 14:6 NIV) God had my attention.

Back in New York

Soon after our talk, I headed back to the airport to fly back to New York. Looking at my life, I shouldn't have had anything to be sad about. I had a great boyfriend who was waiting for me and whom I believed I was going to marry. Peter Bucossi was my first love. From the moment I laid eyes on him, I knew the falling in love part would follow. Peter held my heart with the look in his eyes. I worked in Little Italy as a waitress serving the most amazing Italian desserts and cappuccinos at the famous Italian bakery Ferrara's.

I was standing in the back of the restaurant when, all at once, six to seven of the best-looking, fit stuntmen strolled in. They had just wrapped a movie in Brooklyn. One by one, they passed me on the way to their table. And then there he was. We were face to face when Peter said, "Oh my God." At that moment, we both knew something had happened that was out of our control. More about that later.

I was doing stunt work, and my career as an actress looked as promising as anyone who was just starting out. I was young and still believed all my dreams were going to come true. New York wasn't my favorite place, but now that I had the chance to see my brother and hear the words he spoke, I knew something good was around the corner. Something I could call mine. Something called hope.

The *Very* Good News

Sometimes God shows up at the very last minute. When we think we've lost His attention and He hasn't heard a prayer, light shines in the dark, and He grabs hold of our thoughts all over again. Hope is the conviction that there is something more than we can tangibly touch or see when we are in moments of despair. Hope dances with our faith. It is impossible to have one without the other. No matter how great or small our faith in God is, we only need the smallest amount to believe that He will see us through our doubts and insecurities. The *very* good news is that *God comes through when we come to Him.* The outcome may be different than we anticipated, but His faithfulness, like the rising of the sun each day, meets us in every step and far outweighs the depth of our fears.

God comes through when we come to Him.

"Hope deferred makes the heart sick, but a longing fulfilled is a tree of life."

(Proverbs 13:12 NIV)

Chapter 3
The Call

"Every human being is under construction from conception to death."
- Billy Graham

I was living in Queens, NY, with my sister Kim in a cockroach-infested one-bedroom apartment with no air conditioning. I remember getting out of the shower and sweating before I could even dry off in that dingy little bathroom. It was horrible. And oh, waking up in the middle of the night and turning on the light in the kitchen to watch what seemed like hundreds of very well-fed cockroaches scatter. I never did know where they came from. I hated living in Queens, but like most actresses, I had to be ready at a moment's notice for auditions, so Queens it was. At four-hundred-fifty dollars for a one-bedroom apartment in the late eighties, that place was a steal. Eventually, Kim moved out and got on with her life. We loved living together.

Another day had gone by, and there I was, lying in bed at night, about to open the book my brother gave to me. From the beginning, I was pulled in. Story after story, I read about how God changed the lives of people. I read about a football superstar, an Olympic ice skater, and a former counsel to the President of the United States. I read about Andy Pettitte, a pitcher for the New York Yankees at the time. I loved the Yankees, so I was intrigued.

I met Andy years later when I was waitressing at Morgan's Steakhouse in White Plains, NY. I told him his story in the book was very influential in my beginning a relationship with Jesus. He was very gracious. As I kept on reading, I became aware of one thing. Not only did they all talk about God, but they also talked about Jesus. They all experienced the power of God through Jesus, who changed their lives from the inside out. Jesus made the difference. Experiencing Him was priceless. Only Jesus fit into a hole that nothing or no one else could fit inside of. Jesus brought fulfillment to each life, unlike anything or anyone else could bring. Not status. Not wealth. Not the perfect family. Nothing. I wondered how all these people who grew up in different cultures with different life experiences experienced the same exact newness that a relationship with Jesus offered.

The black and white pages started turning into color with every chapter. I wanted to live a life of color. I wanted my life to be red, pink, yellow, and green instead of the lifeless gray it had become. And then I turned the page, and there it was. The words that would make all the difference. The hope I was hoping for was written on the page I was about to read. I read the words, and then I paused. I thought, is this what I have been waiting for? Is this that? So, I told God I tried everything in my life, and nothing worked. Everything I tried brought me no peace and no change personally, emotionally, or spiritually. The perspective I held, held no promise. The high of whatever it was I was anticipating every time fell through the cracks like a lie, and before I knew it, I was out there looking for another lie to believe.

I thought if God was everything He said He was and if Jesus was really the Savior of the world who died to save me, then I have nothing to lose and everything to gain. And, if Jesus was a lie like everything else I tried, then my life would just stay the same. So, I did it. I read the words again from my heart. I still didn't fully understand the gravity of my sinful nature or why Jesus died in my place, or what that meant eternally. Still, I was at a point where I had come full circle, and having exhausted so many avenues, I surrendered.

I turned off the light, closed my eyes, and fell asleep. Little did I know I would never be in the dark again. Hours later, I woke up to a new day.

The sun arose, and so did I from the dark into the light. I can't explain it, but something was different. I was different. It was as if a light had been turned on inside of me, and now I could see. The lightbulb I saw in my vision was no longer over my head but somehow found a way into my heart. I prayed the prayer, and the prayer became alive in me, and everything hard became easy. God found me, and I found hope. I felt like a little girl all over again, like I was given a second chance. Like I was born a second time with a new life ahead of me. No money machine in sight.

I could just see Satan slithering in his skin at the fact that he had just lost one of his captives. I never really belonged to him anyway. I belonged to God, and now I sealed the deal! I didn't know what the days ahead would bring, but I knew at once that the distance between God and me no longer existed. Jesus filled the space, and I was ready to know what the personality of God looked like through Him. I found what I was looking for. Finally, I had hope.

The Cornelius Story

There's a story in the Bible about a guy named Cornelius who lived in a city called Caesarea. Cornelius was a Roman centurion and commander of at least one hundred soldiers. Cornelius feared God in a good way. He did what was right in God's eyes because He cared about what was important to God. He put God first and always made the choice to please God instead of looking to please man. In the book of Acts, Luke tells us, "He and his family were devout and God-fearing; he gave generously to those in need and prayed to God regularly." (Acts 10:2)

Cornelius got as close to God as he could on his own. And I could relate to that. God saw his heart and made the sovereign decision to step into the faith of a Gentile man. God sent Jesus for the Jews first, but when His own people rejected Him, in all of His holy readiness, He sent an open invitation to everyone else in the whole world, known as Gentiles, to *come and see* who he was and to share in the gift of salvation. Jesus was changing the world one person at a time, and the first Gentile he was going to start with was Cornelius. One of the ways God speaks to us today is by giving us visions and dreams, and it was no different two thousand years ago. One day while Cornelius was praying, he had a vision and saw an angel of God who gave him direction. (Acts 10) He sent one of his soldiers to Joppa to get the Apostle Peter, who simultaneously had a prophetic dream regarding the Gentile, Cornelius. Peter wasn't happy about the dream and struggled with God, but God revealed the meaning of the dream, and soon Peter was off to the house of Cornelius, who was waiting on him in his house packed with relatives and friends to hear the message Peter was about to share. Needless to say, Cornelius was the first Gentile who received Jesus as His Lord and Savior. Jesus bridged the gap between God and Cornelius and me. *When we get as far as we can go on our own in our pursuit of God, God goes the distance and meets us where we are.*

> *When we get as far as we can go on our own in our pursuit of God, God goes the distance and meets us where we are.*

Jesus lays down like a bridge and says come and see.

God saw Cornelius just like he sees you and me. He knows where we are and meets us exactly when and where we need Him to show Himself. We don't have to change one thing. All we need is a mustard seed of faith to trust Him. Have you ever seen the size of a mustard seed? He doesn't ask for much. I see now that God had been wooing me all along, from the darkest and most desperate times in my life to the moment I gave my life to Him. It was like He was throwing me breadcrumbs that, unbeknownst to me, I was following, but they weren't enough. I wanted the whole dang Italian loaf of hot, crusty bread fresh out of my mother's oven with butter drooling down my chin. All my life, He was after my attention. He never let a moment go by without my wide eyes, wondering if He could see me. If He was really watching every move my stumbling feet were making, somehow, I thought He could. Jesus said, "No one can come to me unless the Father who sent me draws them, and I will raise them up at the last day." (John 6:44 NIV)

God is always in the background filling the holes in our lives with truth so that one day when we look back, we will see He was always there. How we respond is up to us.

Jesus called me to follow Him, and I said yes.

The Audition Call

The phone rang, and I answered the call. It was Jim Lovlett, a stunt coordinator in town. After he introduced himself to me and we had some small talk, he asked me if I was interested and available to double as a no-name actress in a low-budget movie that was going to shoot in September. We talked a bit more, and I said I was open. He gave me the address to the production office on the west side so I could meet some folks and leave my resume. I wasn't the only one who was up for the job. Before we hung up, he said, "Oh, and the name of the movie is, Dirty Dancing."

I hung up the phone and immediately thought, oh no, what have I just done? I had been a Christian for about five months, and there was no way I could work on a movie with that name. I didn't know what to do. I thought I'd just call him back and tell him I had a change of heart, but I didn't want to make a bad name for myself in the business. And what would my reason be? I couldn't tell him the truth, and I wasn't going to lie. Who writes a movie and calls it Dirty Dancing, anyway? I slept on it and decided to stick to my commitment and just go. I left the rest up to God. If I was meant to get the job, I'd get it, and if not, that was fine with me. Whatever the outcome was God's will.

I got the job. I was going to be Jennifer Grey's stunt double in Dirty Dancing.

The *Very* Good News

God sees you. He sees you reading this book right now. He knows what your thoughts are before you say one word. He knows what your struggles are and where your incompetence lies. He knows how your sweet victories cling to your heart. He knows when you've gone as far as you can go and can't go anymore. God loves you right where you are and continues to say come and see who I am. He says, just when you think you know all about me, I am going to show you more. I am the one who created you, and I am the only one in the whole world who knows you better than anyone else. The *very* good news is that God is saying there is no need to look any further. I am who you have been searching for. I am true love. Open your heart and let me in, and together we will have a blast at the good life.

"For God so loved the world that he gave his one and only Son, that whoever believes in him shall not perish but have eternal life. For God did not send his Son into the world to condemn the world, but to save the world through him."

(John 3:16:17 NIV)

Chapter 4

Broken Hopeful

"The Christian life is not a constant high. I have my moments of deep discouragement. I have to go to God in prayer with tears in my eyes and say, 'O God, forgive me,' or 'Help me.'" - Billy Graham

Following Jesus was fun. It was like having a make-believe friend who wasn't make-believe. Jesus wasn't a stranger to me. He was more than a historical figure. I took Him literally. He was believable, and I began to believe *in* Him. The author of Hebrews said, "And without faith, it is impossible to please God because anyone who comes to Him must believe that He exists and that He rewards those who earnestly seek Him." (Hebrews 11:6 NIV)

I only needed a small amount of faith to please God. Still, it seemed to work because my faith in Him kept on getting bigger. As I put my faith in Him, God, in return, would put *God. Put. His. Faith. In. Me.* more of His faith in me. Soon I had bundles of faith hidden in my heart for every day of the week!

God. Put. His. Faith. In. Me.

God trusted me to follow Him. Where I lacked in faith, He gave me more. He didn't just leave me with the small amount I had. He believed in me to use the faith He gave me and do something with it. To walk out of darkness into lighted unknown areas. To move with hopefulness through moments of despair. To love where I had hatred sown within my heart from wrongs done against my own good. To places of unforgiveness, I had to take a good look. Charles Spurgeon says, "Faith goes up the stairs that love has built and looks out the windows which hope has opened." *Faith and action beg for physical, emotional, and spiritual movement.* I had to put God's faith in me into action, or it would be rendered useless.

Faith and action beg for physical, emotional, and spiritual movement.

We started to become this team. Me and Jesus. It was perfect. In the beginning, we had a relationship just like it was supposed to be before Adam and Eve messed up and let greed get the worst of them. I began to talk to Jesus out loud. And when I wasn't talking to Him out loud, I heard that not only could He hear my thoughts if I didn't speak them, but he even knew when I was going to sit down and get up. That is crazy! Who does that? God does. And I have proof from a King named David, "You know when I sit down and when I rise up; You discern my thoughts from afar." (Psalms 139:2 ESV) I was beginning to have the faith of King David. However imperfect, King David was an amazing man of faith, and when I say I was beginning, I mean I was barely grasping the start of an immense call on my life to live with an unbreakable faith. My imperfections rose to the surface of my heart with grace enough to slowly mull over the sin in me. God deals with us gently according to his mercy. I was up for the challenge but far from the goal.

Soon after I accepted Jesus, I met whom I call my spiritual mother, then Sandy Perrill, now Sandy Stratton. I was bartending at a restaurant on the upper eastside when I met Sandy. Sandy was a waitress, and one weekend, she saw me reading my Bible behind the bar. I had one of those tiny ones that only had the New Testament. Sandy asked me if I was a Christian. I responded that yes, I had just recently become one. That started a life-long friendship and sisterhood in Christ. Sandy needed a place to live for a few months until she was ready to move to California, where I later moved to become her roommate. Today, Sandy and I are family. I couldn't imagine my life without her in it! She had a way of explaining the thoughts in my mind when I would read something in the Bible that I didn't see eye to eye with.

I wouldn't want to be in my head if I was Jesus. I wouldn't want to put anyone through the ups and downs of my depression and anxiety, especially Him. Slowly, I started to believe that He not only knew my thoughts but also deeply knew me to the very core of where He now made His home. How He could live in the dusty cruddy corners of my heart, I don't know. I should have cleaned it up before He got there, but I didn't know how, nor did I know how dirty it was until now. The good news is that we don't have to change one thing to come to Him. He promises to make all the changing in time.

I heard about this holy thing. Like getting holy and being this holy person now because God was holy. I had no idea how someone like me could possibly be holy with my past, but I had to leave that up to Him. Supposedly, He takes broken things in us and makes them new. He takes us through a personal and spiritual refining process, and eventually, we become this shiny new thing. This change happens deep down and is a step toward this becoming more like Him and less like us. It had to do with obedience. *Conviction of sin causes obedience to God, and obedience to God causes slivers of holiness that shine through the scarred places of our wrongdoing.* If there was someone I wanted to become more like, it was Jesus. I was learning how loving and compassionate He was. How forgiving and just He was, too. There was a woman named Mary Magdalene who had seven demons that she was delivered from and the Samaritan woman who was living in sexual immorality, both of whom Jesus didn't reject. And there was this guy named Saul who persecuted the Christians. He was the worst. He even stood there and watched one of Jesus' followers, Stephen, get stoned. He later became the Apostle Paul.

35

Jesus loved all of these people unconditionally. If God could change them, I believed He could change me. I believe God can change all of us. We have to give Him permission. And I love that.

If He could look at me and see something good to work with, that would be a good thing. I guess that's why God called himself the Holy Spirit because He was making us Holy like no other spirit. I guess He could have called Himself the happy Spirit, but I suppose He cared more about our becoming holy than our becoming happy. Anyway, isn't being happy subjective? But joy, on the other hand, is something different. That's something I needed to work on. But that's another book.

I loved reading the Bible. I couldn't put it down. I read it when I woke up. I read it on the subway. I read it in the waiting rooms of auditions. And I read it before I went to bed each night. I read the whole thing from Genesis to Revelation. I didn't understand everything and had questions, but my ignorance didn't stop me from wanting to know and learn more about God.

I dove in head-first and, over the years, grew fins strong enough to swim against the current. And I mean against the current. The ways of Jesus were different from the ways I was living. Needless to say, there was a huge learning curve ahead. Jesus talked about giving us a helper called the Holy Spirit, and when I said yes to Him, He put His Spirit in me, who was Holy, to guide me through life so I could start to make good and right decisions in His eyes. I was told that this is where the Holy Spirit comes in to help me divide the truth from the lies. To help give me wisdom and understanding. I couldn't say that I loved Him yet. I mean, I was just getting to know Him. I was reading all about Him, but it took some time for His Words to sink in.

I dove in head-first and, over the years, grew fins strong enough to swim against the current.

Jesus spoke words of truth. His spirit depicted holiness, light, and love. Jesus said it like this: "If you love me, keep my commandments. And I will pray to the Father, and He will give you another helper, that He may abide with you forever—the spirit of truth, whom the world cannot receive, it neither sees Him nor knows Him; but you know Him, for He dwells with you and will be in you." (John 14:15-17 NKJV)

Rejecting the Holy Spirit is detrimental to our eternal life. Jesus was the truth, and this is a hard fact. Life is not about your truth or my truth apart from the truth that is of God. There is one truth to follow, and that truth is found in the one true and living God, whose name is Jesus Christ. Followers of Christ follow Christ. Followers of the world follow the world and its ways. The truth leaves no room for interpretation. The thing is, Jesus gave His life for everyone in the world. He left no man or woman out of His salvation plan.

Christianity is all-inclusive because Jesus died for everyone. However, it is exclusive because Jesus is the only way to God. Jesus died for every human being. He died to deliver order back into our lives. Not in our order. His order. I wanted to learn who the one true living God was and why He sent Jesus to die for the world so He could save it. And why did He have to save the world? From what? I wanted to know why everyone who accepts Jesus in their hearts shares an inner feeling that is quite unexplainable. I can only describe it as being born again. I wanted to know what made the God of the Bible different from every other god. I wanted to know more about eternity. Before we leave this world, I learned that God gives each of us a personal invitation to accept Him into our hearts. We are all faced with this serious decision, and I pray we all choose Him.

There was a man named Nicodemus who came so close to acknowledging Jesus as King. We don't know if he became a follower of Jesus in his lifetime, but some question if he was a closet Christian. I think he was. After Jesus dies on the cross, Nicodemus is at His burial. Nicodemus was a Pharisee, a prominent member of the Sanhedrin (government), and a teacher of Israel. He was curious after hearing about Jesus and knew God had to be with Him, not realizing that He was God. He had previously arranged to meet with Jesus late in the night so no one would see him with Jesus. He had some questions he needed answers to. The Apostle John tells the story,

Now there was a Pharisee, a man named Nicodemus, who was a member of the Jewish ruling council. He came to Jesus at night and said, "Rabbi, we know that you are a teacher who has come from God. For no one could perform the signs you are doing if God were not with him." Jesus replied, "Very truly, I tell you, no one can see the kingdom of God unless they are born again." "How can someone be born when they are old?" Nicodemus asked. "Surely they cannot enter a second time into their mother's womb to be born!" Jesus answered, "Very truly I tell you, no one can enter the kingdom of God unless they are born of water and the Spirit. Flesh gives birth to flesh, but the Spirit gives birth to spirit. You should not be surprised at my saying, 'You must be born again.' The wind blows wherever it pleases. You hear its sound, but you cannot tell where it comes from or where it is going. So, it is with everyone born of the Spirit." "How can this be?" Nicodemus asked. "You are Israel's teacher," said Jesus, "and do you not understand these things? Very truly, I tell you, we speak of what we know, and we testify to what we have seen, but still, you people do not accept our testimony. I have spoken to you of Earthly things, and you do not believe; how then will you believe if I speak of heavenly things? No one has ever gone into heaven except the one who came from heaven—the Son of Man. Just as Moses lifted up the snake in the wilderness, so the Son of Man must be lifted up, that everyone who believes may have eternal life in him." For God so loved the world that he gave his one and only Son, that whoever believes in him shall not perish but have eternal life. For God did not send his Son into the world to condemn the world but to save the world through him. (John 3:1-17 NIV)Having much to think about, Nicodemus parted. The scholar Jon Paulien writes, "Christian tradition suggests that Nicodemus gave evidence in favor of Christ at the trial before Pilate, was deprived of office and persecuted by hostile Jews as a result, and was ultimately baptized by the apostles, Peter and John." Nicodemus had a one-on-one with Jesus. A face-to-face meeting in the dark for fear his peers would see him and hold it against him. He was a man of stature and wealth in town and, at the time, could not see giving his position up to follow a person who called himself God.

In my humble opinion, I believe Nicodemus regrets his non-response to following Jesus on that night. He shows up at the burial site with myrrh and aloe, and I believe he mourns time lost with the Savior of the world. He may not have given his life to Christ for peer pressure, but in his heart, he wanted to, and could it be that he actually secretly did? Maybe, it was when he was all alone. Perhaps, he didn't even tell His wife. I wonder. I have plenty of regrets in my life, as we all do. But I didn't want to regret not giving God a chance to show me who He really was on a level I could never understand apart from Him. Nicodemus, like you and me, was not promised tomorrow. Thankfully, he was given a life long enough to possibly receive salvation. The bottom line is that none of us know the number of our days to be lived here on Earth but God. When we're out of here, we're out of here, and we do not get a second chance to say I'll give it a shot now. I'll try you out, Jesus, and see if we make a good team. Nicodemus lived in Jesus' time and feared acknowledging Him in the public square. He didn't confess with his mouth that Jesus is Lord, to Jesus' face, and not to those in his inner circle. If you find yourself being drawn to God on an intimate level, I pray that you say yes to the call. Say yes, to Jesus today because you don't know if you will wake up tomorrow. You don't even know what will happen to you when you walk outside your door today. *Don't risk the regret of waiting too long because you think you're owed time that may not be yours.*

Don't risk the regret of waiting too long because you think you're owed time that may not be yours.

From the time of Nicodemus' secret meeting with Jesus to His crucifixion and burial was a long period of personal introspection for him. *God's timing is perfect, and He works through*

God's timing is perfect, and He works through time, preparing our hearts for outcomes that secure our place in time.

time, preparing our hearts for outcomes that secure our place in time.

Answered Prayers in Front of a Production Office

It seemed like forever since Peter and I went our separate ways. Though God revealed to me that we weren't meant to be married, it took me years to accept. In one of our last conversations, before we split, Peter wondered how he would know that we weren't supposed to be together or that it was over. He said something to the effect, "Will I see you on the street someday and just know?" I said, "Yes. If that's what you believe, then yes, that's what God will do."

It was mid-week or so when I grabbed a picture and resume and hopped on the subway to head into the city. Production offices were always in the town's most remote and dingy places. Guess the rent was cheap. The subway dropped me off blocks away, and I had a bit of walking. As I walked toward the office, I saw someone walking toward me. I knew it was him. Love doesn't fade so quickly. Even throughout the years, it pops up like an old clown from inside a music box convincing you you've made the worst mistake in your life by letting love go as the melody to The Way We Were plays over and over. Love has a way of bouncing around like that in and out of a heart. We were the only two people on that cold city street. I'll never know, but chances are he had come from the same production office I was headed to drop his picture and resume off. We stopped and had some awkward, small talk, and both went our separate ways. I turned to look back at him, walking away; that was the last time I saw my first love. I believe that was when God answered Peter's prayer, and he knew he didn't love me anymore. On that day, I believe Peter's sky was made clear blue. I walked away, too, knowing he was set free. I was happy and sad. Now I had to finish letting go. It took years.

The Stunt Work Begins

It was time to fly out to North Carolina, where Dirty Dancing was filming. I met Jim for the first time at the airport. Once we were up in the air, Jim gave me the script to read so I could look over the scene we would be shooting. Every new job came with new pressure. Would I be good enough? What if the director didn't think I was the perfect double? Would the stunt coordinator like the job I did? What if I couldn't do the stunt? How dangerous was it going to be? You were always remembered for your last stunt job, and you might not get another one because of it. I hated having to prove myself every time. The stunt community was small and cliquey. Everyone wanted to be a stunt person except me. I never woke up and decided I wanted to be a stunt woman. Never. Thanks to Peter, I fell into it. No pun intended.

It all started when I was living in Gramercy Park, pursuing acting. There was a stunt coordinator, Frank Ferrara. Frank was very persistent in asking for my picture and resume. There weren't many stuntwomen who were my size and who could double a lot of actresses. I was the perfect height and weight. At the time, there was only one stunt woman the same size, and she became busy all the time. I wasn't interested and never gave him a resume, but that didn't stop him. One afternoon when I was hanging out at home, the phone rang, and it was Frank. He said, "I need you on set right now." I said, "What do you need me to do." He said, "Don't worry. Trust me." So, I headed to the location on the west side highway. The movie was called F/X, and I was the stunt double for an actress named Martha Gehman. Before I knew it, I was wigged and wardrobed to look just like her. I was riding shotgun down the west side highway, harnessed to the back of a van and driven by a crazy stunt driver. That was my first movie. Before F/X wrapped, I got hired to do another movie called Sweet Liberty, and the ball started rolling.

My Experience on the Set

It wasn't long before I was at Lake Lure, North Carolina, in a small, hot, sticky dance studio rehearsing on a balance beam for a scene we were about to shoot the next day. Jim would peek his head in to see how things were going. This was the room where the dirty dancers rehearsed as well. The crew and I would play hacky-sack in the parking lot between rehearsals. I wasn't very good at it, but it made me sweat. Those white jeans I had to wear were a bit tight, and I could stand to lose a last-minute pound.

Soon the sun set, I settled into bed, and it was time to shoot. I got wigged and wardrobed, and then I waited, and I waited some more. When Jennifer finished her scene, it was my turn to pick up where she had left off. I was walking to set, and I took my mark, and—you guessed it—I waited!

The director yelled, "Three, two, and…" the music began to play. I had no idea I was about to dance to the greatest scene in my life and that most of the world would come to know. Patrick Swayze pointed his finger at me, inviting me to come and join him on the log.

For a time such as this, I felt that no one could walk across that log and dance with Patrick except me. And no one could walk the road I was on toward Jesus except me. I had to get closer to Him on my own. I wished it was easy, but it was hard listening to demons breathe down my neck every day, whispering how unworthy, undeserving, and unlovely I was. But when I made a commitment to follow Jesus, He made a commitment to be there for me too. That was a good thing!

God told Jeremiah, "You will seek me and find me when you seek me with all your heart." (Jeremiah 29:13 NIV)

And Jesus said to those who followed Him, "Ask, and it will be given to you; seek, and you will find; knock, and the door will be opened to you." (Matthew 7:7 NIV)

He was never going to leave me alone, and I wasn't going to turn around now, no matter how bad I felt about myself. The road I was on was a narrow one, and Jesus was becoming very real to me.

Although the way was narrow, there was only one way to get across that log, so I had to find the courage inside to put one foot in front of the other and hope I didn't fall too short of the job I was called to do. With music blaring, excitement reeling, and Patrick grinning at the scene, I lifted one foot up and placed it in front of the other, and then I lifted the other foot up and placed it in front of that foot, and the dance began.

The *Very* Good News

Our time with the Lord is sacred and not to be missed. It is holy, not to be fooled with. The Lord is saying spend some time with me so I can get to know your heart. I already know everything that is in your heart, but I want to hear it from you so I can encourage you where you are. Spend some time with me so I can show you my heart. Together we can turn the world around. Together we can twirl around and swirl around in all the things of life. But I need you to spend some time with me because it all happens there; the miracles, the answers, the clarity, the revelation. When we are together gazing into one another's eyes, life unfolds. And the dreams, oh, the dreams I have laid out for you, are waiting for you to step into in the timing of my perfection. If you only knew. As you get to know me, you will realize the *very* good news is my heart for you, and my dreams will become your dreams, and there won't be any confusion as to the direction of your life.

"See, I am doing a new thing! Now it springs up; do you not perceive it? I am making a way in the wilderness and streams in the wasteland."

(Isaiah 43:19 NIV)

Chapter 5

Knives Are For Cutting...Me

"Beware of no man more than of yourself; we carry our worst enemies within us." - Charles Spurgeon

Every step I took in my life always went back to the sexual abuse and how I felt about myself. Satan planted his seed in me when I was a child, and I felt his lies growing in me every day since. I believed I was bad. I was a bad thing, and some days were unbearable. When the pain got to the point where I couldn't take it anymore, I took the solution into my own hands instead of placing it in God's hands for holy healing. I listened to the voices in my head and not the written word of God. I believed the lie instead of the truth. I was self-destructive in the worst of ways. I only tell the following story, for the redemption that followed years later was greater than the mutilation itself.

The blood was everywhere, on the sheets, on the floor, in my hair, on my pretty little ugly face. I need a needle this time and some thread.

My father shouts on the other end of the phone, his voice cracking in panic. "Denise! NO!"

"Denise, you have to love yourself." I hear the words of my mother in the background.

But how could I love what is unlovely? How could I love the failure that I am? If she only knew it was the set she gave me that I used. 'If she only knew' fills me with sorry.

I was a cutter.

The Mind of a Cutter

On my bad days, it was as if a balloon was about to burst inside. I was going to implode. There was no place to house one more breath of worthlessness and self-hatred, so I began to slice a sliver of skin to let the air out slow and steady. Anxiety could not hold me captive in my own body anymore. I was my own prisoner, and I had to set myself free from the pain in my heart. Tears fell, and I was fixated on what I needed to do. I would begin to tap the blade on my wrist skin. "You can do better than that," I'd say, "so get going." And then, with one hard nab, flesh cries red. "Good," I say, "Don't stop." I get more aggressive, as if I will win a trophy for the best cut. The more blood I see, the better I feel about myself. "Good girl," I say. The cutting turns to a violent stabbing ripping skin, wishing my heart was dead. Trance takes over, and blood spits on my clothes and face. Anxiety is released, and the balloon in me shrinks. I have made room for me to breathe again, in and out, again. The pain in my heart is now displaced in my body. The frozen tears stop, and what is left of the pain drips backward up my face and slips back into my eyes. I am tired. I close my mind. I've had enough for one day.

I soak the washcloths in warm water and clean the blood before it gets hard on my skin. I reach for the band-aids and a long sleeve shirt for a hot summer day. I always had band-aids on hand, especially the really big ones.

Cutting was a way to keep feelings to myself—a way to suffer in silence and put Jesus back on the cross. I was afraid. I was always afraid and always looking for love. Real love. The God kind of love only found in his son. Jesus loved me, but I didn't love him. And I didn't love him enough to take care of His Holy Spirit who lived in me. I wanted to walk with Him, but I didn't know how to tap into the ability within myself to do that. God was very patient with me and the mess I had become. Suffering was an everyday event in my mind, whether alone or in a crowd of people. It's a part of the Christian life. Jesus suffered for us so that with Him, we would be able to find a way through our pain. He was sent to stop the suffering that Satan started in the Garden. Suffering hurts. With a passion for Jesus, Pastor Steve Berger states, "Suffering doesn't disprove God; it affirms His reality and validates His word! The fact that people even recognize good and evil goes all the way back to the Garden of Eden...it is in our very eternal DNA. The fact we love and long for what is good and ache over that which is wrong and produces suffering is proof of our Creator's existence and our longing to return to what we had before the fall...and most don't even realize that!"

My Experience in the Log Scene

I saw Patrick waiting patiently for me on the log. It was as if he had this gift he couldn't wait to give me. I walked slowly toward him, almost testing him to see if he was really going to be there when I reached him. Would he take my hands and lead me walking backward on that thing? How could I trust him? I took my time, step by step, not knowing what my destination would bring. If I fell, I'd only have myself to blame. Stunt people take their lives into their own hands.

Could I trust giving everything to Jesus? My fear of never amounting to anything or anyone? My dreams that still haven't come true? My hope to find a guy to love me for who I was and to be there no matter how messed up I was? You know, the for better or for worst thing? Over the years, I never realized how much I was holding back. I wanted to trust God all the way, but I didn't have anyone walking with me to teach me how to do that. And I didn't have a church at the time. I had a handful of great friends, some of whom never knew how dangerous my behavior toward myself could become, but they didn't live nearby.

I have a best friend from childhood. Her name is Kathy. She's married to John and has a daughter, Jessica. I love Kathy. I call her Stef. She always checked in on me. She cared and always went the extra mile for me. She came and visited me when I needed her most. It's funny how friends are there, and then they go away. I always felt I wasn't the friend to Kathy that she expected of me. Maybe I wasn't good enough? Perhaps I didn't meet her needs as a friend. How could I? I was too engrossed in my weaknesses; I hadn't the strength to look outside of my own situation. I didn't mean to be so selfish. I was just sad. Not just sad, very sad. Like when Jesus made it a point after he created the universe and said it wasn't just good, but it was very good. Or before he makes a point to those he was teaching and says, 'Very truly, I say to you....' It's the 'very' that makes us listen harder. Maybe we simply took different paths in life for a time. Whatever our differences are, our hearts always have and always will bring us together.

One day I got to thinking that if Jesus rose from the dead and now is in me, I can rise up from whatever dark thing it is that weighs me down. I wondered whether Jesus hurt when I cut myself. Could He feel the knife ripping into my skin like when those roman soldiers struck him that day walking up that hill to die on a cross for me? I dig deeper. Jesus allowed the Pharisees to cut him and let his blood drip out of His body, in His hair, on His face, and in the dirt.

Jesus was cut.

I say it again, Jesus was cut!

I remember when Donna told me, "Jesus was cut, so you don't have to!" That's it! That's the answer! Jesus is the answer!

Jesus. Was. Cut. So. I. Don't. Have. To!

I put the knife down for good. I lay the pain and the depression and the worthlessness and the lies and the self-hatred and every unholy thought at the cross. I glue myself to planked wood stuck in holy ground. I look up with the wind pulling tears from my eyes, and I repent for hurting Jesus. Paul, who was one of Jesus' followers, writes, "Do you not know that your body is the temple of the Holy Spirit within you, whom you have from

God? You are not your own. You were bought with a price. So, glorify God in your body." (1 Corinthians 6:19-20 ESV) I wasn't exactly glorifying God when I was cutting myself. I was glorifying Satan.

To all you cutters out there: How dare we hurt Jesus when he was hurt for us! I grieve in guilty shame and beg God for His forgiveness. Remember, Satan's goal is to kill you and me; he will go to every extreme to do that. He wants us gone. Dead. Even if you don't have a relationship with him yet. Something tells me that you will. And the cutting of ourselves is proof that something bigger than our pain is dying to come out and live in the light. Something in us wants to live and tell our story, which is very powerful and threatening to Satan. There is that word, 'very,' again! We have to go beyond the knife and take our stories to the *very* ones who have lost their voice.

The spirit of shame often accompanies those of child sexual abuse. And it lingers for years. Shame immobilizes us and keeps us hidden behind a state of unworthiness. When I look back on my cutting days, I can see clearly that there was a demon working in and through me. The act of cutting came from a thought in my head that I listened to. The only way the devil can get to us is through our minds. He cannot enter a heart. The mind is extremely powerful and is a demon's only entryway. He knows our weaknesses, so we must always be alert and learn how to fight his evil thoughts off. John instructs us, "…the one who is in you is greater than the one who is in the world." (1 John 4:4 NIV) It is clear that some spirits come directly from hell and Satan himself, and others come from Heaven and God. John also tells us, "Dear friends, do not believe every spirit, but test the spirits to see whether they are from God because many false prophets have gone out into the world." (1 John 4:1 NIV) Jesus would never encourage any of us to cut ourselves, but Satan is all about it.

God strictly tells us that cutting is not an option for anyone. The book of Leviticus states, "Do not cut your bodies…I am the LORD." (Lev. 19:28 NIV) Jesus is our way out of temptation. I pray He delivers us all from evil.

The Bible Cutter

There's a story in the Gospel of Mark about a man who cut himself. Jesus was traveling with his disciples when they met up with a demon-possessed man. Mark writes:

> They went across the lake to the region of the Gerasenes. When Jesus got out of the boat, a man with an impure spirit came from the tombs to meet him. This man lived in the tombs, and no one could bind him anymore, not even with a chain. For he had often been chained hand and foot, but he tore the chains apart and broke the irons on his feet. No one was strong enough to subdue him. Night and day among the tombs and in the hills, he would cry out and cut himself with stones. When he saw Jesus from a distance, he ran and fell to his knees in front of him. He shouted at the top of his voice, "What do you want with me, Jesus, Son of the Most High God? In God's name, don't torture me!" For Jesus had said to him, "Come out of this man, you impure spirit!" Then Jesus asked him, "What is your name?" My name is Legion," he replied, "for we are many." And he begged Jesus again and again not to send them out of the area. A large herd of pigs was feeding on the nearby hillside. The demons begged Jesus, "Send us among the pigs; allow us to go into them." He gave them permission, and the impure spirits came out and went into the pigs. The herd, about two thousand in number, rushed down the steep bank into the lake and drowned. Those tending the pigs ran off and reported this in the town and countryside, and the people went out to see what had happened. When they came to Jesus, they saw the man who had been possessed by the legion of demons, sitting there, dressed and in his right mind; and they were afraid. Those who had seen it told the people what had happened to the demon-possessed man and told about the pigs as well. Then the people began to plead with Jesus to leave their region. As Jesus was getting into the boat, the man who had been demon-possessed begged to go with him. Jesus

did not let him, but said, "Go home to your own people and tell them how much the Lord has done for you, and how he has had mercy on you." So, the man went away and began to tell in the Decapolis how much Jesus had done for him. And all the people were amazed. (Mark 5:1-20 NIV)

One of the amazing things about this story is that once the man was delivered of his demons, he wanted to follow Jesus. He wanted to go with Jesus. But Jesus knew he would be of better use in his town, sharing the good news of his deliverance and leading others to Jesus. Just like Mary Magdalene and the Samaritan woman, this man also, once delivered, wanted to follow Jesus wherever He went. *Our demons keep us from being set free from lies into the truth. From the point at which we act out the very thing that we have been fighting is the point when we are possessed by a demon spirit.* It is the demon that takes possession and acts out. I believe my great uncle was possessed by a sexually immoral, impure, and perverse spirit when he abused me. If he were delivered of his demons, it never would have happened. I was a child when I learned that he had died, and I never cried. Later in my adult life, I had to go through the process of forgiving his heinous sexual acts on me. He had a variety of wicked schemes at hand.

The Apostle Paul tells us to be strong and shares how to fight the fight of faith when Satan comes against us in the battle of our minds:

> Finally, be strong in the Lord and in His mighty power. Put on the full armor of God, so that you can take your stand against the devil's schemes. For our struggle is not against flesh and blood, but against the rulers, against the authorities, against the powers of this dark world and against the spiritual forces of evil in the heavenly realms. Therefore, put on the full armor of God, so that when the day of evil comes, you may be able to stand your ground, and after you have done everything to

stand. Stand firm then, with the belt of truth buckled around your waist, with the breastplate of righteousness in place, and with your feet fitted with the readiness that comes from the Gospel of peace. In addition to all this, take up the shield of faith, with which you can extinguish all the flaming arrows of the evil one. Take the helmet of salvation and sword of the Spirit, which is the Word of God. (Ephesians 6:10-17 NIV)

Today, when I feel the spirits of suicide or any unworthy spirit come over me, I use a bigger knife. It's a sword. A sword that points to the truth about how much God loves me. And when the hissing serpent aims his lying tongue at my weakened spirit, and my confidence gets shaken, and my faith crumbles to dirt, I pick up my sword and wave it high as heaven. I scream for JESUS, JESUS, JESUS at the top of my lungs. Get behind me, Satan! I stab strong and mighty at the lie, puncturing it smack in the middle. I steady that cross on holy ground; I thank God for the resurrection of Jesus, and I rise.

The *Very* Good News

Jesus says, I stood before a jeering crowd about to be condemned to death. I took up my cross for you and began my long, agonizing, and painful walk to Calvary. I was brutally beaten to the point of unrecognizability, with blood running from my body. Do you get the picture? It's important that you do because if you don't, we can't move forward. I was cut, so you don't have to, and by my strips and lacerations, you are forever healed. Do you get it? I sure hope so. You are my beloved, and the *very* good news is that if I had to do it all over again for just you, I would. You are worth every drop of blood I shed on that day. Remember that! But I did it to save the whole world. Now, stop and go; tell that to the mountain!

"But he was pierced for our transgressions; He was crushed for our iniquities; the punishment that brought us peace was on him, and by his wounds we are healed."

(Isaiah 53:5 NIV)

Chapter 6

Falling Short, Gaining Ground

"A dark cloud is no sign that the sun has lost his light; dark black convictions are no arguments that God has laid aside His mercy." - Charles Spurgeon

With every step, I was getting closer and closer to Patrick. I felt as though I could feel his excitement calling out to me like a mighty wind circling around me. Every eye on set was on my feet, inching my way to him. His sheepish grin was seeming to whisper "hey baby" under his breath. The music was playing in my head when we met on that log. Face to face, we stood ready to take on the dance of a lifetime. A time we would remember forever after the fact. I looked into his hungry eyes, and we danced! Right there with the cameras rolling and the lights shining like a scene out of heaven.

We danced! It felt as though we were so lost in the song that we had no idea what was happening around us. That's what movies make you do, but when you're in the movie, and you forget you're in the movie, there's nothing like it. Finding true love and wanting to keep it is a magical thing, even when we're pretending!

I began to trust Jesus, and even though I couldn't physically see Him standing right there in front of me, I knew He was there. Although I still had much fear to work through personally, I began to trust God and was less afraid of following Him wherever He wanted to take me. Moses states, "It is the LORD who goes before you; he will never leave you or forsake you. Do not fear or be dismayed." (Deut. 31:8 ESV)

To open my eyes and see him face to face someday was like a dream I had anticipated. Imagine Jesus looking into your eyes. How would that make you feel? Free? Guilty? Sorry? Excited beyond belief? Regretful? Maybe all of those things.

Forgiveness

Sometimes I wish I could do it all again. The dance with Jesus from the very beginning when I discovered His presence on that morning in Queens, NY. I know I can't go back in time, but what I can do is start fresh right now. Today, all over again, with Jesus. I am thankful that He doesn't let me go or throw me away like a piece of dirty trash every time I sin and let Him down. Every time I let myself down. Every time I need to ask Him for forgiveness, He forgives me just like He says we are supposed to forgive one another. Peter asks Jesus how many times we are supposed to forgive one another. He thinks seven times is undoubtedly enough. Jesus had a different answer, "I tell you, not seven times but seventy-seven times." (Matthew 18:22 NIV) The bottom line is that we are called to forgive one another endlessly, just like Jesus forgave us endlessly when He gave His life and forgave us of our endless sins. There isn't a limit when we talk about forgiveness. Not only does Jesus forgive, but He forgets our sin and never holds it against us. That's pretty great! If only I could forget as He does. I'm working on it. I think the key is to pray for those who do us wrong.

Jesus isn't like a friend or a family member who writes you off because you have a different perspective on world issues. Jesus is in the business of forgiving, and so am I, even when it's hard. *Unforgiveness holds us back to the point where our relationship and growth* *Unforgiveness holds us back to the point where our relationship and growth with God are stalled. It's a dangerous game to allow our pride and arrogance to get in the way of forgiving others.*

56

with God are stalled. It's a dangerous game to allow our pride and arrogance to get in the way of forgiving others. We should not want to be caught putting our belief systems over the word of God. We will never top the truth. *Our version of light will always dim in comparison to the truth of God's word.*

> Our version of light will always dim in comparison to the truth of God's word.

Christ Shines.

Jesus died for us and not the other way around. We need Him. He doesn't need us. He gave himself to us as a sacrificial offering to make right all that had become wrong since sin entered the world. In her book Seven Prayers That Will Change Your Life Forever, Stormie Omartian said, "Forgiveness doesn't make the other person right, it makes you free." Forgiveness sets us free to live life unhinged by the deeds of others against us. *Forgiveness takes maturity. And when done well, partnered with humility, it binds those involved together rather than separates them.* Jesus said clearly, "For if you forgive other people when they sin against you, your heavenly Father will also forgive you." (Matthew 6:14 NIV) Paul even tells us as a follower of Jesus, "Bear with each other and forgive one another if any of you has a grievance against someone. Forgive as the Lord forgave you." (Colossians 3:13 NIV) If you're unsure if you have unforgiveness, just check your anger. Unforgiveness and anger go hand in hand, and pride usually holds the team together. Where there is one, most likely, there is the other.

> Forgiveness takes maturity. And when done well, partnered with humility, it binds those involved together rather than separates them.

Paul addresses anger, "In your anger do not sin; do not let the sun go down while you are still angry, and do not give the devil a foothold." (Ephesians 4:26-27 NIV) Anger, if not dealt with, will give way to a hardened heart. The author of Hebrews tells us, "Do not harden your hearts as you did in the rebellion, during the time of testing in the wilderness." (Hebrews 3:8 NIV) We must remember that Jesus deliberately died for every human being, and throughout our lives, whether we confess to be a follower of Him or not, He is always trying to get our attention in the grandest and smallest of ways. In the end, He wins, and the world will lose. When in question, He is always right, and the world is always wrong.

Me and Patrick

There we were, Patrick and I, dancing along steady and strong, and the thing we feared happened. In the fun-filled fantasy, my objective shifted. I began to lose my balance because I took my eyes off the prize. Sometimes circumstances in life have a way of moving our focus from what is a priority to what is mere survival. A scary place to be. We are all made for more than just survival.

A Hospital Stay

There was a time in my life when the lights dimmed to the point where I couldn't see the truth anymore. I wasn't giving God the place He rightly deserved. As a matter of fact, I gave Him no attention at all. Not a safe place to be. Not ever. I let the whims and woes of life lift me far from the stability and security I once found in my faith and landed myself like a swirling tornado in a hospital room hooked up to tubes flushing out every dark memory.

It was the fourth of July, and there were no fireworks sparkling around in my heart. Rather, my head was full of drab gray, having to live a life of unrequited love and unrealized dreams, coupled with esteem lower than imagined. It happened more than once, but this time my spirit couldn't grasp what holiness meant. It was buried in rejection so deep there was no light in sight. I was stuck under dirt and didn't have the strength to fight my way up. It was hard to breathe.

So I grabbed the Tylenol and the beer. And then some more Tylenol and some more beer. And that's how the day went down. With no defense at hand and all hope gone, I reached for the only weapon that was familiar and a sure guarantee of relief. I held the knife and began to puncture the skin.

I swore I would never again. But, at that moment, I forgot what I knew.

Satan has three things on his to-do list every day, all day; *to steal* every breath in me, *kill* every ounce of hope I could muster up, and *destroy* my will to live. And he was certainly focusing on all three on that day. I couldn't even remember or consider the familiar warning of hope from Jesus. "The thief comes only to steal, and kill and destroy; I have come that they may have life and have it to the full." (John 10:10 NIV)

It took me years to realize the danger of letting my guard down and find hope in knowing what my right was as a believer. I was eligible for spiritual armor and spiritual weaponry that worked to keep the evil one at a distance and sometimes gone for good. Jesus told me about this authority I have in His name, "I have given you authority to trample on snakes and scorpions and to overcome all the power of the enemy; nothing will harm you. However, do not rejoice that the spirits submit to you, but rejoice that your names are written in heaven." (Luke 10:19-20 NIV)

I called Tommy. He was always there for me. He heard the pain in my voice every time and came running, just like a best friend.

After feeling like I had been in a dark trance for three days, I woke up on the third day. I didn't feel well. My organs were gurgling inside of me, and I knew something was wrong. I called Tommy, and he told me I needed to call Vanderbilt Emergency Room and tell them what I did. So, I did. The woman on the other end of the phone listened intently, and without legally being able to give me any information, she advised me to come down immediately.

Patty and God's Perfect Timing

My friend Patty was on her way over. We had plans to have a girl's day out. When I opened the door to let her in, she knew something was wrong. She had a gift of seeing through me. We were like family in that way. I filled her in as to what I did and that I needed to go to the ER *now*. There was no time to waste. She drove me. Once we arrived, I filled out the necessary paperwork, and we waited for what seemed like forever before my name was called. I sat down with a woman who went over my information and asked me what I had done in depth.

I'll never forget what she told me. With grave certainty, she said, "You incurred a slow death." That didn't sound good to me, even though I hated living. Maybe I had some hope after all. Honestly, I had a deep feeling that I would pull out of this, and it would all be ok. I wasn't sure how yet. I wasn't trying to kill myself, but I didn't care if I died either. The years caught up with me, and I was numb. I don't remember praying. I was so far gone in my black hole that I believed I would always live unloved, lonely, and never good enough for anyone or anything.

I hate Satan.

I see now that I was exactly where he wanted me to be. He takes advantage of our brokenness on every level. I was almost dead, and he loved the thought of stealing time away from me here on Earth. He knew that if I got my crap together, I would be a massive threat to him and knock him off of the throne of my heart. Did I write that? It looks like I am going to have to take a good long hard look at what I just admitted to. I'm not going to edit it because I think it's true and something we all need to think about at different times in our lives.

Whom are we serving? Satan? God? Ourselves? Why am I giving Satan privilege to my inadequacies and shortcomings when God threw him out of heaven because of his shortcomings? Satan was without humility. Why had I let him take advantage of my weaknesses when I had a loving God who promised to strengthen those weak places? Why did I allow myself to believe my dreams were impossible to grasp when I served a God who said all things were possible? Why would I believe God didn't have the power to calm the storms that raged all around me when He walked on the waves? And, why in the world would *Our faith will fail us when we flirt with fear.* I ever admit that *I can't* do this or that when God said, *I can* do all things through Christ who strengthens me." (Phil 4:13 NKJV) *Our faith will fail us when we flirt with fear.* Who do I belong to, anyway? C. S. Lewis reminds us, "Hardships often prepare ordinary people for an extraordinary destiny." And I was certainly going through a hardship. It was time for me to realize who accepted me and whose power lived in me when I accepted Him. I was slowly beginning to color inside the lines. It's funny how we wait to be noticed until one day, we notice no one really cares or sees us, and we move on.

My First Out-of-Body Experience

I'll never forget it. It's as if it happened yesterday. I was in therapy at the time, trying to figure out why I didn't want to live. It was a painful time. No real healing was taking place. I guess I was trying to find a way out of the dark place I was in. I cried a lot, and I was scared a lot. I had a fear of abandonment too. When I was a little girl, my brother Bobby was like my protector. I always loved when he'd come home after being gone for some time. I loved having him around. I loved him so much. I still do. When I was a kid, I used to jump on his hip, wrap my arms around him, and rest my head on his shoulder. I'd sit there safe and sound. It was perfect. I felt protected when he was around. When he was tired, he'd put me down. I don't know how old I was. Pretty young, I suppose.

Healing is like walking around with an empty suitcase. You keep emptying your heart and mind out, and then the great waiting of restoration begins. It takes years to get filled up with the good stuff. And you sort of stand in place with your eyes staring up, hoping for a sprinkle of rain to wet your faith. It's hard not knowing exactly where you're headed to. So, between the therapy and lugging an empty suitcase around, I had this thing happen to me one night.

I was in my bedroom in North Hollywood, and it was not quite dawn. I was somewhere between sleep and awake when I felt my body start to vibrate. From head to toe, this electric feeling was all over me. Then slowly, I felt what I believed was my spirit lift from where I was lying and then go back down in me. And it kept happening until suddenly it shot up to the ceiling and saw myself lying on the floor. I had just moved and didn't have

61

a bed at the time. I was petrified.

Looking down at myself, I saw that I was trying to move my body, but I couldn't. I tried with all my strength to move and wake up, but I couldn't. I had no spirit. It was on the ceiling. I guess you can't move without a spirit. I mean, I didn't know what else it could be. My bedroom door was slightly open, and all of a sudden, I saw six of the most grotesque heads floating into my room. They had no bodies and were attached to each other like a blob. They were all laughing at me as they kept getting closer and closer to me.

Then I saw my mother and father walk through my bedroom door to where I was lying. They stood behind the headboard, and my mother said, "I think she's going to be okay. She's going to make it this time." I remember thinking what am I going to be okay from?

At that point, the demonic heads were laughing harder and harder and getting closer and closer to me. They repeated, "We got you! We got you now!"

There was nothing good about what was happening. It was very demonic. It was an attack straight from hell. On the way to getting better, the demons come out and play hardball. Any bit of light I began to see was soon met with darkness.

I had to get out of there, but I couldn't move or speak and couldn't wake myself up. I remember a story a friend told me who had out-of-bodies all the time. She said she thought the name of Jesus. So, I tried to call out to Jesus, but I still couldn't move my mouth. I tried again and again, but my lips were frozen shut. So, I thought, if I can't speak the name of Jesus, I will think of the name. And I did.

I said the name of Jesus to myself over and over and over again. I thought of the name Jesus for what seemed like one million times.

And then, finally, the six heads started backing off. They dissolved out of my room and backed out the door. My spirit on the ceiling returned to my body, and I woke up.

***

I was lying in a bed in the ER with tubes flushing toxins from my tired, frail body until a room opened up. Patty was there. We called my brother Tommy. He came quickly. I put him through a lot. How he always worried about me but had a way of letting things go at the same time. Tommy loved me, and I never felt like he ever judged me. I never judged him either, and I never will. It's not our place to judge. I will leave that up to God. The doctor came inside the curtain where Tommy and I were and explained how we would know when my organs were shutting down. He said I would begin to forget what I was just told and forget my own sentences and repeat myself. Soon enough, those things started to happen. Tommy asked if we should call Mommy and Daddy. I said, "Yes." My parents packed a few things and headed for Nashville from Manahawkin, NJ.

The Next Morning

The nurse made her rounds throughout the evening. I didn't sleep well with tubes hanging out of me. I'm not a back sleeper. I made it through the night, though. I knew I would. Something told me it wasn't my time to go. I believed God wasn't finished with me down here. I was still trying to master the art of loving myself that my mother begged for me.

Someday, Mama. Someday.

A new day began, the sun was as sunny as it always is, and I was alive. After a couple of hours, my doctor came into the room with a team of interns. He said to them, "People that do what this girl did die. Why didn't she die?" I lay there listening to them, throwing out different medical scenarios about why I was alive. I know there was a medical reason, but I was focused on the spiritual. He should have asked me because I think I was the only one in the room with the correct answer. Without a shadow of any doubt, I knew there was only one way I was still breathing and headed in a good direction.

God.

Period.

It was God and God alone who saved my life. God is sovereign and can do anything he wants at any time in anyone's life. He brings life, and He brings death. It's all in His timing. Over the years, I grew fond of one Scripture I applied to many instances. Now that I am a Christian, it pertains to me. The Apostle Paul put it perfectly, "And we know that all things work together for good to those who love God, to those who are called according to His purpose." (Romans 8:28)

Even in this incident, God was going to make something good come out of it. All because I love Him, and He has called me according to what He has meant for me to do in my life. He makes ugly things beautiful. Tearful times joyful. If you believe, he changes people like me and you into living, giving vessels of hope for the entire world to learn from, grow from, and get through.

To this day, I believe one of the reasons God kept me alive was because Tommy was with me the night I jumped off the ledge, so to speak. And I believe he would never have forgiven himself if I died when he could have taken me to the ER that night. I always wondered about that. I think he does too. God loves Tommy so much that He would never put him through the guilt of that. I was such a rebel at that point that I wouldn't have gone anyway. I thank God for loving me.

After about ten days in a psych ward, because that's where they make you go when you pull a stunt as I did, I was released to go home. I hated being there, but I did teach myself how to use watercolors. I even painted a picture for my mother. When she went to heaven, I made sure I had it. It's hanging in my kitchen.

God gave me a second chance at life, and I tried to take advantage of it. I felt alive like I hadn't in years. Even though I still drank my wine every night or went to happy hours with friends after work, I was beginning to lean into my spirituality again. I was still a Christian, and everyone who knew me knew I was the one they could come to if they wanted to talk about God or pray. I loved praying with people anytime, anywhere.

There was a time when I couldn't remember not having a bottle of wine in my house every night. Now, I can't remember the last time I had a glass of wine in the house. Over the years, the depression came and went, and I was on and off medication. Nothing really worked like when I first got on Prozac back in the nineties. Two weeks to the day, I saw the sun in my sky for the first time. I couldn't believe I started to feel like everyone else. I was definitely late to the party. But that eventually wore off, too. Not the party, the Prozac.

My walk with Jesus was still a little slippery, just like my dance with Patrick. So many disappointments made it hard to refocus.

The DUI

One night, Leslie Matkosky, another friend, and I went to the Bluebird in Nashville to hear her husband, Dennis play in the round. From *Maniac* from the movie Fame to *I Need You* by LeAnn Rimes to *You'll Think of Me* by Keith Urban, Dennis was a favorite. Being a songwriter, I loved listening to talented songwriters play their songs, sometimes more than the artist who cut the song. And don't get me started on writing songs—another disappointment. After getting so close to songs getting cut by Trisha, Martina, and Faith, I started to think it shouldn't be so hard to get a song cut if you were doing what you were called to do. But I didn't stop writing at that point. It was after I had two songs that were going to be on a Michael Jackson tribute record that never came out when I hung up my hat. The funny thing is, I still think I have one good lyric left in me! I never did know what happened to the publishing deal Ron Stuve was working on for me.

We shared three bottles of wine that night in a very short time. I drank most of it singing to *Red Light*. Those nights usually only lasted a few hours, and I never stayed later than the last song was played. We said our goodnights and walked to our cars. Leslie asked if I was ok to drive, and I said yes.

What was I thinking? I wasn't.

The truth is, I drank and drove all the time. So did most of the people I knew, but that didn't make it right. I just never got caught. I deserved a DUI years ago and more than one. I don't understand why God waited until now, other than His favor was on me. I believed it would have been the next time that would have been catastrophic. Like so many others, I never thought I wasn't ok to drive or that a DUI was in my future.

Don't. Drink. And. Drive!

I was not putting God first in my life on that night. Most of the Proverbs in the Bible were written by King Solomon, one of which states, "Trust in the LORD with all your heart and lean not on your own understanding; in all your ways submit to him, and he will make your paths straight." (Proverbs 3:6) Needless to say, I was not putting my trust or looking to the Lord at all those days. I did not lean on his guidance for anything and certainly didn't ask Him if He thought it was okay for me to drive after drinking so much wine. I was drunk, but if there was anything I was sure of, it was being able to get myself home. Don't let the deception of alcohol fool you.

I only lived a few miles away. I headed down Harding like I always did. It's a straight shot with a couple of stop signs. The operative word there would be 'stop,' and I didn't. I was the only one on the road, or so I thought. Seconds after I drove through a stop sign, blaring red lights from out of nowhere kissed my bumper. I pulled over, and I knew it was over. I knew my life was about to change for a long time.

I'll never forget that night. It was the night when I fell very short of God. I was reminded of how much I wanted to serve God. All I ever wanted to do was tell people about God and be used by Him, and now I have ruined everything. Surely God wasn't going to use me anymore. I felt hopeless. My spirit was torn.

The Turning Point on the Log

Something began to happen in the midst of Patrick and I laughing and swirling around on that log. With all the excitement, we lost our balance and almost fell. It all happened so fast that I don't even think the crew and, certainly, Emile Ardolino, the director, noticed how we quickly came back from it. Immediately, Patrick reached for my arms and ran his hands down to my hand, and held them tight. We both froze where we were. The cameras kept on rolling, and we kept holding on to one another. I know what I was thinking, but I wonder what Patrick was thinking. In that one merciful, miraculous moment, Patrick did what I believe God intended for him to do. Patrick looked at me and spoke the words that would eventually begin to change my spiritual life.

"Don't look down. Look at me. In my eyes."

"Don't look down. Look at me. In my eyes."

And so, I did. I looked into Patrick's eyes, and he looked into mine. It was more than magical to me. It was miraculous.

God used Patrick in that moment to move me straight to the heart of Jesus.

A force of strength poured over us from the waterfalls of heaven's grace that we both found within one another. It was as if no one else on that movie set was there—no cameramen, no director, no props, not even the log we were standing on. It was just Patrick and I, suspended in mid-air in Lake Lure, North Carolina. I felt that nothing could stop our stare. It was as if we were caught in the moment of recovering from a near miss, and we were going to pull this balance up from our toes all the way through that pin at the top of our heads, and heaven was going to lift us back to regain our balance. Only the powers of heaven can do a thing like that.

Only God can do the impossible when giants are breathing down your neck. You will fall into the evil clutches of the devil once again, and there will go not only your faith but possibly your life. I mean, the script did make mention of the sharp-edged rocks below. It was as if God reached His hand out and lifted my heart chin, and asked me to trust Him. Filming the log scene that day was a pivotal point for my walk with God.

The *Very* Good News

God is saying, I know you're sad, but you've come so far. I know where you began because I was there too. I didn't leave you where you were. Look back, and you will see me with you. Do you notice me? That time when you were crying on your couch. When you were driving in your car? I came to you and pulled you out from the darkest holes of your life. Do you remember that? That was me who pulled you up and out from the pit. I sent your friend. I gave you the money. I held you tight in the night when you wanted to die. I kept you alive. It was me all the time. Me. It was me who put your feet on solid ground even though you never gave me credit. I am the rock you stand on, whether you realize it or not. I am He. I have no substitutes. Stay by my side, and the *very* good news is that I will blow your mind and show you great and mighty things that you do not now even know.

"The LORD is close to the broken-hearted and saves those who are crushed in spirit."

(Psalm 34:18 NIV)

Chapter 7

The Act of Balancing Faith

"We weren't meant to be somebody – we were meant to know Somebody."
- John Piper

I was almost four months into my DUI when God began to get my attention like never before.

For one year, I had to drive around with an interlock device in my car that I had to blow into every time I started the engine to prove that I wasn't drinking and driving. It was awful, but I deserved it, and it was a lesson I will never forget. Not only did I have to blow in it to start the engine, but every few miles while driving, it would beep, and I would have to blow in it as if I stopped and drank along the way to work or wherever I was going. It was a bit ridiculous. I wasn't that kind of a drinker, nor was I an alcoholic—well, I don't think I was. However, I did drink more than I should have. But the law is the law, and I had to pay the price for my reckless behavior.

It had been a long time since I remembered God speaking to me personally. You know, like I was one of His kids whom His eye was on. I thought, if I can't go to happy hours with my friends for one year, I'll drink at home. And I did. For weeks I would always make sure I had a bottle of wine in the house. I poured that Cabernet as if it were Penguins grape soda like when I was a kid. That stuff was so good. So was the orange flavor. My mother bought it from the Grand Union in town. Mr. DeBellis was the store manager, and he hired me to work at the register. I loved my job, and I loved him. He was the best boss I ever had. Mr. DeBellis believed in me and had a way of getting me to believe in myself. He passed a few years back. If only I knew he was here at Vanderbilt hospital, just minutes from where I lived, I would have visited him. One night, God began to speak to me as I was gulping down a glass of wine and watching whatever was on TV. I wasn't seeking Him, but He seemed to think it was a good time to talk to me. The good listener in me propped up. I was feeling a bit lonely and sad. Depression was still my best friend, and it reared its ugly head a lot during my time alone at home. I always heard that God speaks in a still, small voice, and that night, I believe I heard Him. He started to speak in the silence of my living room while I minded my own business on my over-stuffed denim couch. In the sweetest, most convicting, loving voice, He said, I want all of you. I am a jealous God, and I don't want to share you with anyone or anything anymore. He continued, I want the depression and the loneliness and the anxiety. He kept on going like a role call; I want the unworthiness, the shame, and the self-doubt. He didn't stop there.

He said, "I want the fear."

He had me at "fear." I put the glass of wine down and began to cry. That was the kicker. How could He see me in my living room? How did He know how I felt deep down? I wasn't even thinking about those particular things in that moment. Was He sitting on my couch with me? Or standing in the corner near the screened-in balcony? Could it be that my heart was yearning to take its snug place with God no matter how bumpy the ride gets? Could my heart be making a turn in the right direction without consulting me?

Charles Spurgeon wrote, "Have your heart right with Christ, and He will visit you often, and so turn weekdays into Sunday's meals into sacraments, homes into temples, and Earth into heaven."

I was starting to look forward to what God was about to do in my life. No matter where He was, He saw me. God was there, somewhere, and somehow He got a good look at the state of my heart. Maybe He just saw everything from the inside of me, from the place I buried Him over the years. Perhaps I made room in my DUI life to give Him a chance to rise up in me. Just maybe. When I accepted Him in my heart, He placed His seed of life in my heart. At that point, His promise to never leave me began. He planted His love for me deep in the walls of my heart, and his love in me began to grow. God is faithful to Himself even when we are not faithful to Him. God can't let His own word down.

During those days locked in at home, I began to look at what sin is. I found this beautiful summary in Randy Acorn's book, Grace: A Bigger View of God's Love.

What is sin?

It is the glory of God not honored.

The holiness of God not reverenced.

The greatness of God not admired.

The power of God not praised.

The Truth of God not sought.

The wisdom of God not esteemed.

The beauty of God not treasured.

The goodness of God not savored.

The commandments of God not obeyed.

The justice of God not respected.

The wrath of God not feared.

The grace of God not cherished.

The presence of God not prized.

The person of God not loved.

That is sin.I had a lot of homework to do.

The Samaritan Woman

I was reminded of a story in the Bible about Jesus meeting the Samaritan woman at Jacob's well. In that day, the Jews were not permitted to be seen with a Samaritan, let alone speak to them. Jesus was with His disciples on His way to Galilee from Judea. Jesus decided to pass through Samaria first. (John 4:4) Jesus was tired from his journey and sat beside the well around the sixth hour of the day, which was the hottest time of the day. Jesus sent His disciples ahead of him.

Most women go to the well to get water early or late in the day when it is cool. The Samaritan woman was an outcast in her own town because of the sexually immoral life she led. So, she came to fetch her water when no one else was there to scorn her. Not only was she married five times, but she was presently living in sin with her boyfriend. *Going to the well when the other women weren't there was her way of hiding her sin and, at the same time, allowed her to continue to live with an unrepentant heart.* Jesus sent the disciples away on purpose because Jesus had work to accomplish. Jesus was drawn to the Samaritan just like the Samaritan woman was drawn to the water in the well. Jesus was intentional about His visit, and soon He engaged in a conversation with the woman. Jesus asks the woman for a drink of water and responds to her,

> "If you knew the gift of God and who it is that asks you for a drink, you would have asked him, and he would have given you living water." (John 4:10 NIV) Jesus tells her

that He is the Living water. Jesus is whom she needs. Jesus continued, "He told her, "Go, call your husband and come back." "I have no husband," she replied. Jesus said to her, "You are right when you say you have no husband. The fact is, you have had five husbands, and the man you now have is not your husband. What you have just said is quite true." "Sir," the woman said, "I can see that you are a prophet." "I know that Messiah is coming (he who is called Christ). When he comes, he will tell us all things." ...Jesus said to her, "I who speak to you am he." (John 4:1-26 NKJV)

Jesus broke all cultural barriers on that day. He knew soon He would die for the sins of the world and that His death would encompass all ethnicities, races, and cultures. Not only would the sins of the Samaritan woman be forgiven, but mine and yours would be forgiven, too, by His finished work on the cross.

I made a choice that day that changed the trajectory of my life. I never knew getting drunk was a sin until God revealed it to me. Little by little, throughout my walk with Him, He would reveal truths to me like this one. It's called the sanctification process. *God removes the rough edges in a heart that longs to follow Him.* It's becoming holy because He is holy; it takes a lifetime to achieve the end results. Paul tells us, "And do not get drunk with wine, for that is debauchery, but be filled with the spirit." (Ephesians 5:18 ESV) I got to thinking. I never read anywhere in the Bible that getting drunk makes you a better Christian. It leads to all sorts of things we would never do while sober. The author of Proverbs also reminds us, "Wine is a mocker, strong drink a brawler, and whoever is led astray by it is not wise." (Proverbs 20:1 ESV) I held on to Jesus like I never did before.

Not only did Jesus find me at a low in my living room, but He knew everything about me. He knew what I was battling deep down before I really knew. It's like He took the time to open my heart's eyes to see what only He could show me. He knew the reason I was trying to fill my empty soul with wine and anything else I could. He knew I was at the end of myself. Like the Samaritan woman, I was tired of hiding my sin. He loved me enough to find me and save me from one more night out on the town, which could have cost my life or possibly someone else's. That is something I could never have lived with. Never. God saved me in His perfect time. I was thankful then, and I am thankful now.

The Bible talks about God disciplining us because He loves us. The author of Hebrews says it like this, "...the Lord disciplines the one he loves, and he chastens everyone he accepts as his son." (Hebrews 12:6 NIV)

Jesus accepted me as his daughter when I accepted Him in my heart in that Queens apartment, and throughout the years, amid my lowliness and sinful heart, He never let me go. He remained faithful to His word and kept on loving me. However, I, too, never let Him go either. Although I went through periods of falling short of what He had called me, I never denounced the Holy Spirit. And I never turned my back on Him to follow a false god. I never will. The truth, who is Jesus, has literally set me free from entertaining the thought of falsehood pertaining to who the true God is. That's why I'm writing this book. It's for you, not for me. I began to regain faith as Jesus' truth balances me.

From the time we accept Jesus, He is all about tearing down and building up from the inside out. He has a much better version of our heart homes than we do. In Mere Christianity, C. S. Lewis writes:

> Imagine yourself as a living house. God comes in to rebuild that house. At first, perhaps, you can understand what He is doing. He is getting the drains right and stopping the leaks in the roof and so on; you knew that those jobs needed doing and so you are not surprised. But presently, He starts knocking the house about in a way that hurts abominably and does not seem to make any sense. What on Earth is He up to? The explanation is that He is building quite a different house from the one you thought of – throwing out a new wing here, putting on an extra floor there, running up towers, making courtyards. You

thought you were being made into a decent little cottage: but He is building a palace. He intends to come and live it Himself.

Back on the Log

What seemed like hours was only seconds before Patrick and I regained our balance and slowly loosened our grip. Fingertips were sliding off fingertips. There was a moment when we looked at each other one more time as if to say, "Are you ready?" We knew we had this. We knew we were safe. We knew we were carried on the wings of eagles.

I put my faith in the one who was bigger and bolder and stronger than either one of us. I began to regain my faith as Jesus' truth balanced me. I trusted the music, and with arms stretched out, we began to shake ourselves silly. I was off like a ballerina in a love scene dancing on a log! *I lifted my right foot and crossed my left ankle, and I twinkled my happy toes around and around and around!*

I lifted my right foot and crossed my left ankle, and I twinkled my happy toes around and around and around!

And like a perfect scene in a perfect movie, the music played loud, the dirt danced as if an earthquake had struck it, and the water bubbled up happily against those rough rocks below. And there went the squiggling of the hips and the flapping of the arms. And so, we danced, and we pranced, and our faith laughed out loud on that day.

The *Very* Good News

If I could put my joy inside your heart, I would. Joy comes from you while you praise me. Joy bubbles up inside of you. Don't turn me off. I am not a faucet for you to turn on and off. Wake up in the morning and praise me. For your feet, wake up in the morning and praise me. For the sun, wake up in the morning and praise me. For the bed you get to sleep in and the pillow for your head, praise me. Praise me all day long in the great and small things, for nothing is out of the question. I never want you to stop enjoying me. Fill your cup to overflow. Remove yourself and your feelings and go ahead and praise me in those moments. Praise moves you from the darkness into the light. Pursue joy and watch me move deeply. The very good news is that joy is just a praise away!

"Be joyful in hope, patient in affliction, faithful in prayer."

(Romans 12:12 NIV)

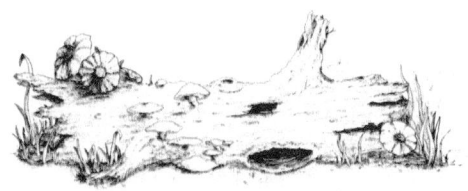

Chapter 8
Finding Grace

"Each life is made up of mistakes and learning, waiting and growing, practicing patience and being persistent." - Billy Graham

Just like it was at the beginning of my walk, I began to have a hunger for the things of God again. I still felt ashamed for what I had done and didn't feel comfortable attending church. Looking back, I see how Satan, the enemy of our souls, will use our past against us to keep us from moving forward in faith. I started watching Oprah's Super Soul Sundays. It worked for a while, but it wasn't the message I was looking for. I wanted the Gospel message. I wanted the truth. I wanted Jesus. I didn't want other religions that appeared to be something you could choose as long as it *worked for you* outside of the God of the Bible. I found it more confusing than consoling. I found it spiritually dangerous for the one who may stumble upon the channel while lost and looking for something to believe in.

There is only one choice when you are looking for True spiritual love.

One Sunday, my desire to be in church again was greater than my sense that I was underserving and unworthy. For years I had heard of a church on the outskirts of Franklin called Grace Chapel. Time and time again, I heard how special this church was. How once you enter the doors of this church, your life will never be the same. Funny how God sets things up. When I moved back to Nashville in September of 2009, I rented a room from Andrea, whose friend Heather was the daughter of the Grace Chapel pastor. However, I was oblivious to the beauty of God's sovereign timing flickering before my eyes.

I knew Grace Chapel was the first church I wanted to visit. I was ready to rededicate my life to the Lord and find a church to feed me spiritually. And so, Grace Chapel it was.

Grace Chapel

I never thought of myself as a farm girl. A barn girl. I always longed for ocean waves crashing against my heart, softening the ridges deep. The smell of the salt and sand sticking on the ocean dripping skin. How peace ripples sacred into my spirit when I stare out into the vast unending of God. How the mountains crumble away in the small of me.

It's funny how God remembered the prayer of a little girl who only wanted to help people when she grew up. And later in life, when that young girl *first believed,* God kept safe her purest desire to help and now to lead people to the truth she found in Jesus.

I find myself in that little girl, *still.*

Only God could have brought those scuffed-up boots of mine full circle. From the backyard of my heart, through every thundering storm, to the very *special* barn doors of Grace Chapel in Leiper's Fork, TN.

I'll never forget that Sunday in August of 2013 when I kicked those barn doors open with these boots and sat myself down in the middle of that glorious place.

I was a bit messy that day.

First, I heard the guitars strum and the drums beat, and then the voices sang out songs with a servant's heart about them. And then the rising from the cushions we all went. Arms stretched wide past our doubt, and hands reached high above the fear of letting go. Our fingertips skimmed heaven's floor and brushed against the hem of Jesus' robe. You could almost feel the swoosh, the restoration.

Faith lifted us toward the blessed hope of forgiving grace. It was as if the sacred blood seeped into our spirit pores, the healing began, and happiness was about to follow.

And how God parted the red seats in that place, so we all could walk down that rug through our shame and our fear and all of our ugly into the promised land of prayer.

When I heard that Pastor preach the Bible from that burnt pulpit up there, my heart leaped. I felt a spirit limb snap back into place back into the vine. I felt living water gush into me, saturating the spirit drought.

This guy's good, I thought.

When that service was over, I marched those broken boots straight up to that burnt holy wood to tell him so.

With mascara tears and head down, heart up, I composed myself like sheep do when they come back into the fold. I didn't know I was out of the fold for so long until that moment. Not really.

"What's going on?" the Pastor asked.

Through trembling lips and with a sniffled pause here and there, I said, "I've been looking all over this place for a church that preached the word of God uncompromised, and I found it today. Thank you. I found where I belong."

From that day forward, every Sunday, I sat smacked down on one of those red seats, and I listened crazy hard to that barn preaching pastor from that burnt pulpit God gave him.

Steve Berger. That's his name. God uses him to unwrap the gift of grace better than any gift on Christmas morning.

Grace is a gift for life.

I thought about getting this guy some knee pads for all the falling and the preaching on the knees thing he does. At least once every Sunday, down he goes preaching in prayer. Compassion for Jesus oozes out of him. And I wonder how many ripped knees his wife Sarah has had to stitch up through the years.

Sadly, due to pastoral changes within the walls of this place, I no longer attend Grace Chapel. However, for eight incredibly life-changing years, God planted my heart inside those barn doors, and today, I speak a little louder. I stand a little stronger. I strut a little bolder.

Today, I am still standing on solid ground.

Free to Dance

I felt as though Patrick and I were finally free to dance in the confidence that we were being watched over and protected along the way. Each step led us closer to safety. And we danced our way to solid ground—in the same way I did with my faith in Jesus dancing through the years. Looking back, I see Him holding my hand all the way. I knew we were always walking down the same road, but where there was once a distance between us and several exits that I took, apart from Him, now we are in the center of that road, holding hands and walking in the same direction. I no longer fight His will.

When our desires are God's desires for us, we will have the desires of our hearts. Why do we fight against what is best for us? Why do we think we know better than God? Why do we believe we have a better way to manage through the hard days in life? Why do we have to be right? Why do we insist on taking a bite of that fruit that is rotten to its core? Why do we have to learn the hard way? I'll tell you why...pride. It all boils down to our pride, wanting more than what God has offered to us through His only son, Jesus, that He led to the cross to die for our sins.

Patrick and I made it to solid ground in Dirty Dancing, and so did I in my personal life. But will you? Will you make it to solid ground with me? I hope so.

The *Very* Good News

God is saying I've waited so long for you to come home. The angels are dancing in heaven, and the party has begun. Now that we are together again, I will hold you so close that you will never let me go. That is not up for negotiation. I love you too much to see you in pain. But when you find yourself in the battles of life, turn to me, and I will be there with you every step of the way. I am your shield and your protector. I am the Savior of your soul, and nothing and no one will change that. So, rest your tired eyes on mine, and let's dance together and fall in love all over again. Your heart is safe with me.

"For this son of mine was dead and is alive again; he was lost and is found. So they began to celebrate."

(Luke 15:24 NIV)

Chapter 9

A Prayer For You

"The greatest kindness one can render to any man is leading him from error to truth." - Thomas Aquinas

The word faith prompts action on our part. James tells us, "For as the body without the spirit is dead, so faith without works is dead also." (James 2:26 NKJV)

Faith walks through every storm we will face in our lives. It does not rest, and it does not give up. Faith, like love, always perseveres and persists until its end is met in triumph and victory. Faith needs you to partner with it. And together, you can change your life and the world. The Bible gives us the definition of faith. The author of Hebrews states, "Now faith is the substance of things hoped for, the evidence of things not seen." (Heb 11:1 NKJV)

And there it is, the word hope all over again. To hope is to believe in something so deeply that someday the thing hoped for will come to a realization. When I took my eyes off my failures and put them on my faith, I began the process of becoming free and living my life in the freedom of Christ.

Through the story of the Samaritan woman, I feel joy. Through the story of Mary Magdalene, I feel the release of unforgiveness and deep healing. Through the story of the man who cut himself, I feel freedom. But most of all, through the story of Cornelius, the very first Gentile to be saved into an intimate relationship with Jesus, I feel hope. Hope for you. Hope that you will take a chance sooner than later, maybe today, maybe right now, to walk out your faith with the one who died for you—just like Cornelius did.

Jesus had you on his mind when He spoke His last words on this Earth, hanging from that Roman cross, "It is finished." (John 19:30 NKJV)

When Jesus took His last breath and 'fell asleep,' His purpose on Earth for which He was sent was complete. And He did it all for love. Jesus died with every sin you and I will ever commit in our lives, and when He rose from the dead, His blood, the blood of the perfect lamb, washed our sins away. And the opportunity for us to be forgiven of our sins was available for the asking. Again, it takes our faith in Jesus to be forgiven so we can begin to live with Him, be redeemed from our past, and start anew.

It all goes back to the beginning. It always does:

- Satan wants to be god.
- His pride gets him thrown out of heaven.
- His first sighting is in the Garden of Eden.
- Adam and Eve believe his lie and fall into temptation.
- Man's perfect relationship with God is broken.
- God sends His only son, Jesus, the lamb of God, blameless, to redeem humanity.
- Jesus lives a perfect and sinless life.
- Jesus takes our sins to the cross.
- Jesus rises from the dead.
- Jesus sits at the right hand of His Father, God.
- His blood washes us clean.

- Through Jesus, we are forgiven, saved by grace, and have eternal life.

- Jesus is the only way to the one true living God.

God didn't leave or reject Adam and Eve because they sinned. He is still their God, but things just got harder on Earth because now they have to live in an imperfect, fallen world that worked its way through time all the way to you and me today. Every human being on the planet is born with a sinful nature because of Adam and Eve. Anything good in us is a gift that is given to us by God.

In the words of C. S. Lewis,

> I am trying here to prevent anyone from saying the really foolish thing that people often say about Him. I'm ready to accept Jesus as a great moral teacher, but I don't accept his claim to be God. That is the one thing we must not say. A man who was merely a man and said the sort of things Jesus said would not be a great moral teacher. He would either be a lunatic -on the level with the man who says he is a poached egg -or else he would be the Devil of Hell. You must make your choice. Either this man was, and is, the Son of God, or else a madman or something worse. You can shut him up for a fool, you can spit at him and kill him as a demon, or you can fall at his feet and call him Lord and God but let us not come with any patronizing nonsense about his being a great human teacher. He has not left that open to us. He did not intend to.God created us with one purpose in mind: to have a relationship with Him. And the only way to restore our relationship with God is through mending our broken one. The only way to do this is to accept Jesus as our Lord and Savior so we can begin a new life guided and directed by His Holy Spirit.

Here is a prayer for you to pray, similar to the prayer I prayed in Buckingham's Power For Living. I invite you to read the prayer and then read it a second time from your heart:

Dear God, I believe that Jesus is Your Son and that You sent Him into the world to die for my sins. I believe that He rose from the dead and is now seated at Your right hand. Please forgive me of my sins; come into my heart and be my Lord and Savior. I give you my life so that from this day forward, I will live for you and not for me anymore. Help me to be more like you and less like me. Amen.

Congratulations! You have become a new creation in Christ, and with that inheritance comes a world of heavenly expectations and excitement ahead. Right here, the process of changing from the old you to the new you just began and that is something to be enormously joyful about! The Apostle John tells us, "Yet to all who did receive him, to those who believed in his name, he gave the right to become children of God." (John 1:12 NIV) You are now not only created in the image of God, but you have just become a child of God! Not everyone is a child of God. To become a child of God, we have to personally accept Jesus into our lives, from which point forward, the benefits of God are released as King David proclaims, "Praise the LORD, my soul, and forget not all his benefits – who forgives all your sins and heals all your diseases, who redeems your life from the pit and crowns you with love and compassion, who satisfies your desires with good things so that your youth is renewed like the eagles." (Psalm 103:2-5 NIV) God will not waste one day in your life; instead, He uses them to your benefit.

Thank you for reading this book. I pray every page from the first to the last was filled with hope that you can hold on to and see the fruition in your life. If you said this prayer, go and get yourself a Bible. You will start to have that same hunger to learn everything about your new best Friend. If you choose not to say this prayer, the Bible will not make sense to you, but if you do, every word will come alive, and you will feel like you were *born again!*

From all the way back to that apartment in Queens to my desk in Tennessee, where I type this book, I share in your new life and promise the best is yet to come. All you have to do is come to God with an open heart and consider Him in everything you do, and He will do the rest.

Becoming a Christian doesn't mean that there will not be hard days, but it does mean that we now have an advocate to help us through those days. It means that even on the loneliest days, we are not alone. It means that when we are faced with a mountain that seems immovable, we can recall the words of Jesus, "For truly, I say to you, if you have faith like a grain of mustard seed, you will say to this mountain 'Move from here to there,' and it will move, and nothing will be impossible for you." (Matthew 17:20 ESV)

Billy Graham states, "Being a Christian is more than just an instantaneous conversion – it is a daily process whereby you grow to be more and more like Christ."

Remember, God is always for you and never against you.

I love you, and so does God. Have a beautifully colored and transformed life in Him, and I will see you in heaven!

XOXO

Denise

The *Very* Good News

Hey, you. That's right; God is talking to you. I waited a long time to reveal myself to you personally. I hope you stay awhile. There's so much I want to tell you about yourself. About your life. I'm going to answer the 'whys' and the 'why nots' and the 'where were you when' times. I'm here to share it all. Now that I have your attention, you will never lose mine. I love you more than you love me right now, and I will never leave your side. Not ever. And the very good news is that soon I will fill your heart with love that is out of this world and comes down from heaven directly from me. I won't overwhelm you learning about me. We'll take small steps together down the road to forever.

"Peace I leave with you; my peace I give you. I do not give to you as the world gives. Do not let your heart be troubled and do not be afraid."

(John 14:27 NIV)

"God of our life, there are days when the burdens we carry chafe our shoulders and weigh us down; when the road seems dreary and endless, the skies gray and threatening; when our lives have no music in them, and our hearts are lonely, and our souls have lost their courage. Flood the path with light, run our eyes to where the skies are full of promise; tune our hearts to brave music; give us the sense of comradeship with heroes and saints of every age; and so, quicken our spirits that we may be able to encourage the souls of all who journey with us on the road of life, to Your honor and glory."
Saint Augustine

Acknowledgments

I thank Jesus for carrying His cross for me. Thank you, for being the only One in my life that has and will always be there for me. Today, I crown You with joyful tears of salvation. It is Your death that keeps me alive and for that I am grateful. I will live out the rest of my days serving You and telling the world about Your gracious love. Thank You for hearing every prayer, wiping every tear, and continuing to be ever so near. Because of You, Jesus, I have overcome obstacles in my life by the power of Your blood and the word of my testimony! (Rev 12:11) I can't wait to see You face to face. I love You.

I thank my mother who is living in heaven for showing me what strength looks like. If I can only master it! I miss you terribly and can't wait for the day when I get to enter into the gates of heaven and wrap my arms around you again. I don't think I'll ever let go. Life down here will never be the same without you. How we use to laugh when I'd tell you stories and you'd say only my Denise. There's a hole in my heart that's full of hope knowing that someday, one day, we will be together again. Thank you for letting me know I could always come home. And, I did! My life wasn't easy, but you saw me through the pain I couldn't explain. I know your prayers reached the very heart of God because I made it through. I love you.

I thank my Father for introducing me to God. As a little girl he would tell us kids to read the Bible. We never did back then. Today, I can't put it down. Because of you, Daddy, the Word of God was introduced to me and now my heart is full of life, love, and hope. I could always count on you to talk to someone that I took home with me when they had nowhere else to go. I'd tell them my Father will talk to you about God and you did each time. I know those moments were life-changing. Your prayers for me manifested a confidence in me to tell my story. Thank you for loving me unconditionally through the rough patches! There were many! I love you.

(My father passed on May 31st, 2023)

I thank my five brothers and sisters, Diane, Bobby, Billy, Thomas, and Kim for seeing me through some of the toughest times in my life. Times I didn't think I would survive. Times when life hurt so much I just wanted to go away. But I didn't and today although, we all live our lives in different places we will always be united by a love that, I believe, will never weaken over time. There's nothing like all of us being in the same room. It's like magic. That's what love looks like. Love looks like the six of us together. Something I can't explain. Something I miss. I love you all and always will.

Thank you to my most amazing sisters and family in Christ, Sandy, Donna, Trish, Kelly, and Leilani. I cannot imagine a day without one of you. You all have been there for me through the hardest and saddest days. No one on Earth knows me better than you all do. To see how far we've all come in the Lord has been one of the greatest treats of my life. Thank you for believing in me, for praying for me, and for standing with me in the faith of our hearts. Your encouragement to pursue my hearts desires helped get me this far. Your faith in me gave me the courage to write this book. I love you all more than words can say.

I thank Kathy Nolan. I will always hold you dear. Thank you for being there for me over and over again! Thank you for having a heart of compassion for me when death was calling my name. Your selflessness made me stronger in a way I can't explain. The way you abandoned everything in your life just to make sure I was OK. Who does that? You do. Our similarities go way beyond our differences and for that my heart is a happy one. I look forward to seeing you soon! I will always love you, Stef.

Thank you, Patty Santostefano for being like a big sister to me. I thank God for using you in my life and for being there at the perfect time. You know me like no one else does! Love you, always.

Thank you, Called Creatives Publishing for believing in my story and giving me the chance to share it with the world. Your encouragement has changed my outlook on the rest of my life. I'm so grateful to be a part of a group of authors and speakers who love the Lord and serve Him with all their hearts. I couldn't be in better company. Thank you Alli Worthington,

ACKNOWLEDGMENTS

Lisa Whittle, Melody Belotte, Morgan Strehlow, Stephanie Kingery, and Ashley Kelly for helping me navigate through the pages of my first book! I'm looking forward to our hard work helping others see themselves the way God does through his unmatched truth of salvation. My love and gratitude to you all!

And finally, everyone else who has been there for me though out the years. You know who you are! Thank you from the most humbled place in my heart. I love you all!

Notes

Introduction

Interview with Larry King on Christmas Day 2005, Billy Graham states, "There are two great forces, God's force of good and the devil's force of evil, and I believe Satan is alive and he is working, and he is working harder than ever, and we have many mysteries that we don't understand."

Chapter 1

Rasmussen, Rebecca. The Bird Sisters: A Novel. United States: Crown, 2011. Pg 128

Chapter 2

O'Flaherty, William. The Misquotable C. S. Lewis: What He Didn't Say, What He Actually Said, and Why It Matters. United States: Wipf & Stock, 2018. Pg. 90

Lewis, C. S.. The Complete C.S. Lewis Signature Classics. United Kingdom: HarperCollins, 2007 Pg 59

Chapter 3

Graham, Billy. Peace for Each Day. United States: Thomas Nelson, 2020. Pg 51

Chapter 4

OKAFOR, KELECHUKWU O.. It Is Written: God's Word in Your Mouth Will Recreate Your World. United Kingdom: WestBow Press, 2011. Pg 25

Quoteslyfe.com, 2022. "Charles Haddon Spurgeon Quotes." Accessed November 22, 2022. https://www.quoteslyfe.com/quote/Faith-goes-up-the-stairs-that-love-1352.

PauleinPaulien, J. (1992). Nicodemus (Person). In D. N. Freedman (Ed.), *The Anchor Yale Bible Dictionary* (Vol. 4, p. 1106). New York: Doubleday

Chapter 5

Rhodes, Ron. 1001 Unforgettable Quotes About God, Faith, and the Bible. United States: Harvest House Publishers, 2011. Pg 201

@pastorsteveberger, December 1, 2022, Instagram post.

Graham, Billy. Confronting the Enemies Within: The Journey Study Series. United States: Thomas Nelson, 2007. Pg 91

Chapter 6

Spurgeon, Charles Haddon. The Saint and His Saviour: Or, The Progress of the Soul in the Knowledge of Jesus. United States: Sheldon, Blakeman & Company, 1857. Pg 52

Omartian, Stormie. Seven Prayers That Will Change Your Life Forever. United States: Thomas Nelson, 2010. Pg. 47

Jaynes, Sharon. When You Don't Like Your Story: What If Your Worst Chapters Could Become Your Greatest Victories?. United States: Thomas Nelson, 2021. Pg 192

Chapter 7

Reed, Rick. Good Stuff for Your Heart & Mind - a Book of Quotes (second Edition). N.p.: Lulu.com, 2016. Pg 203

Threshold: Aperture to the Light of the World. N.p.: Dorrance Publishing, (n.d.). pg 671

Alcorn, Randy. Grace: A Bigger View of God's Love. United States: Harvest House Publishers, 2016. Pg 148

Lewis, C. S.. The Complete C.S. Lewis Signature Classics. United Kingdom: HarperCollins, 2007. Pg. 163

Chapter 8

Billy Graham - IN His Own Words - Plus Free AUDIO Book. N.p.: Raymond Wells, 2022. Pg. 13

Chapter 9

Quoteslyfe.com, 2022. "Thomas Aquinas Quotes." Accessed November 24, 2022. https://www.quoteslyfe.com/quote/The-greatest-kindness-one-can-render-to-1103722.

Lewis, C. S. (Clive Staples). *Mere Christianity : a Revised and Amplified Edition, with a New Introduction, of the Three Books, Broadcast Talks, Christian Behaviour, and Beyond Personality.* HarperCollins edition. San Francisco: HarperSanFrancisco, 2001. Pg 65

Ramsey, Shelley. Grief: A Mama's Unwanted Journey. United Kingdom: WestBow Press, 2013. Pg 101

(God of our life...)

The Holy Bible: New International Version, Containing the Old Testament and the New Testament. United States: Zondervan Bible Publishers, 1988.

Nelson, Thomas. NKJV End-Of-verse Reference Bible, Compact, Red Letter Edition, Comfort Print: Holy Bible. United States: Thomas Nelson Incorporated, 2020.

ESV Study Bible. United States: Crossway, 2

Hotlines

Support Groups and National Networks:

Call the National Suicide Prevention Lifeline at 988 any time of day. The lifeline provides free and confidential support, prevention, and crisis resources for people in distress.

Crisis Text Line – Text HOME to 741741 for free, 24/7 crisis counseling

American Foundation for Suicide Prevention: 1-888-333-AFSP (2377)

Suicide Awareness Voices of Education: 952-946-7998